The Best Parent Is Both Parents

The Best Parent Is Both Parents

A Guide To
Shared Parenting
In The
21st Century

Edited by
David L. Levy

HAMPTON ROADS
PUBLISHING COMPANY, INC.

For information, write:

Hampton Roads Publishing Co., Inc.
891 Norfolk Square
Norfolk, VA 23502

Or call: 804-459-2453
    FAX: 804-455-8907

If this book is unavailable from your local bookseller, it may be obtained directly from the publisher. Call toll-free 1-800-766-8009 (orders only).

ISBN 1-878901-56-7

10 9 8 7 6 5 4 3 2 1

Printed using acid-free paper
Printed in the United States of America

Dedicated to

All the children who could benefit from better parenting and who might yet receive it if our society emphasized parenting half as much as it does sex, money and power.

About Some of the Contributors

Anna Keller is a vice-president of the Children's Rights Council (CRC), Elliott H. Diamond is a co-founder and advisor to CRC, and Alexander Hillery II is an attorney and former researcher for CRC. All reside in the Washington, D.C., area.

Acknowledgements

To Andrew Diamond and Christine English-Martin for their invaluable editing of this manuscript. Also to John L. Bauserman, a vice-president of CRC, for his editing.

The title, *The Best Parent is Both Parents*, is a title from a chapter in Michael L. Oddenino's forthcoming book, *When Kids Come First*.

Table of Contents

Preface
The Best Parent is Both Parents

by
David L. Levy, Esq.
President, Children's Rights Council
January 1993

In 1970, the famed anthropologist Margaret Mead spoke at a seminar call "Sex in Childhood" sponsored by the Children's Medical Center in Tulsa, Oklahoma.

Margaret Mead, the most well-known anthropologist of the 20th century, touched upon many topics in her lecture, including the need to honor the incest taboo to protect children, the need to reduce the incredible violence that pours forth from TV, the importance of breastfeeding babies, and the importance of fatherhood, all topics which are as relevant today as when Ms. Mead lectured two decades ago. We gratefully acknowledge CRC advisor John Money, Ph.D., of John Hopkins University Hospital in Baltimore, for a copy of Ms. Mead's remarks. The remarks, based on a transcription of a lecture given without notes, have never, to Dr. Money's knowledge, been widely disseminated.

An excerpt of her lecture follows.

> We permitted the courts to sever a relationship between a child and his or her biological father. This is something that no court should ever have an opportunity to do. There's no court in the world that can say a brother and sister aren't brother and sister. They can hate each other, they can refuse to see each other; they can call each other names; they can even murder each other, but they are still brother and sister.

> Yet we've permitted the court to utterly deny a father's relationship to the child. We have given the kind of preference to the mother-and-child tie that belonged about 'a half a million years ago' when nobody knew what the father's relationship was. This worked all right then. A man came home to a cave for his supper and sex and looked after the children incidentally, but that was a long time ago.

> We do know something about biological paternity, that the father is the biological progenitor for a child—but we act as if we don't know it at all. As a result, we are eroding paternal responsibility at an appalling rate in this country.

In Chicago recently, we saw the great demonstration of a national association of divorced men who protested that they had no access to their children. This is another social condition—denying a real biological tie. I think one of the things we have to move toward is the recognition that having a child with someone is just as biological as being born from the same mother or being born from the same father.

We're not going to get rid of divorce. People are too badly brought up in too many different ways, and they don't know how to live without other people very well. It takes a couple of tries to find out very often. If we could keep the tie between parents (co-parents who can't live together, but otherwise keep that tie), we would protect children far better than we do now.

There is an incredible emphasis on violence that is pouring out day after day, week after week on television. We have violence between the young and the old, violence between the hard-hats and the hatless, violence between people of different races, violence of all sorts, and this is bearing in upon children and their attitudes toward sex.

We have very adequate demonstrations, I think, in the study of human beings that violence can be substituted for sex quite conveniently and mixed up with sex quite conveniently.

The excessive anger of the Women's Liberation movement is an example of what we're producing in this society. It isn't that we have so much violence in the numbers of people killed, but there have been so many people who enjoy watching them being killed. This is exceedingly dangerous, and the children are being fed on it day after day. It's not necessary. If the community would get it together, it could perhaps, force the mass media to invent some other way of getting people to look at the screen. The advertisers have already discovered other ways. The advertisers now make wonderful ads with nothing but snowdrifts and oceans and stars and everyone sweeps through the air in every direction harmlessly. . .

Now another thing that we've been doing. . .is the extraordinary violation of the rules of incest that have held straight through history. The rules of incest, and every society has them, are one of the most important protections of our humanity. They are one of man's earliest inventions.

They have protected children growing up in the home from sexual exploitations and permitted them to develop love, tenderness and affection, to sit on people's laps and to be put to bed gently, to be bathed and caressed and cared for by adults who would not exploit them, because of incest rules they've grown up with. . .

The stepparent is not regarded as being bound by incest taboos. The result is that the father who marries in a home with a seductive little 11-year-old girl as a stepchild is exposed to the kinds of temptation that he would never have been exposed to in a society that knew what it was doing. Equally, the half-grown son with a young stepmother is everlastingly exposed to all sorts of temptations in regard to their stepsisters.

I'm not emphasizing that either one is worse than the other. I'm just as sorry for the stepfather as I am for the 11-year-old girl, but the fact remains that the protection of children from the exploitation of adults is vanishing in probably well over a million homes in this country.

Margaret Mead provides us with an anthropological perspective, a backdrop against which to focus on an issue of utmost importance to our society today.

Children should not have to "lose" a parent because of divorce, yet courts in America operate on the win/loss principle. One party is declared a winner and the other a loser. As badly as this principle works when the dispute does not involve custody of children, when the issue does involve custody—the win/lose principle is ghastly.

The child did not ask his or her parents to divorce; the divorce is not the child's fault.

Children come into the world with two parents; they should be able to retain two parents, both a mother and a father, if possible, during their formative years. There are situations where it will be impossible to have two living, loving, functioning, parents for a child. But two parents should be the norm, the goal, for children. Why?

Researchers may disagree on many things, but one thing they all agree on is that children generally do better when they have two parents rather than one. Many children of single parents turn out fine, but, statistically, they are more at risk than children with two parents. Children with only one parent are more at risk of getting involved with drugs and crime, of having lower self-esteem, of having alcohol problems, and of being unable to form a lasting relationship of their own when they become adults. They are also more at risk of a variety of other social and mental-health problems.

Divorce affects one million children a year, with long-range negative effects on these children. In addition, about one million children are born of unwed parents each year, and a high percentage of such children will not have even one functioning parent, let alone two.

It took two parents to have a child; it takes two parents to raise the child.

Our society should not expect one parent to do the work of two. If it does, the parent who raises the child is overburdened, while the other parent is under-involved.

What our society has done is to regard the mother as the caregiver and the father as the financial provider. This perception is especially true in divorce, where fathers are not so much absentee parents as they are forced-away parents. They are told that their role is just to provide money, not nurturing.

Custody is still almost automatically given to women. The Census Bureau says 85% of single-parent households are headed by women.

It would not help children to reverse those figures, in order to have most households headed by men, because then children would still have only one parent.

America needs to encourage family formation and family preservation—an intact family with a mother and a father. If divorce occurs, the model of two parents that the child had during the marriage should be what the child has after divorce. This means shared parenting or joint custody—with both parents sharing in raising of the child after divorce.

It does not mean that the parents would have to have a 50-50 split of time with the child, although that might be possible if the parents live near one another. But it does mean that each parent would have liberal access to the child and a share in the decision-making affecting the child's upbringing.

If parents live near each other, shared parenting is easier to work out than if they live at some distance, but even long-distance sharing can work, with a larger block of time in the summer, longer Christmas and spring breaks, and liberal phone access between child and parent.

Our society has not yet recognized the benefits of shared parenting for children of separation and divorce because it has not yet absorbed the research showing that two parents are better than one for children.

But there is hope on the horizon. Both liberals and conservatives have begun to recognize the harm we are doing to our children by denying them the right to two parents.

Both the conservative Family Research Council and the more liberal Progressive Policy Institute said in 1990 that our society needs to emphasize the two-parent family. The Family Research Council talked of a "parenting deficit" and the Progressive Policy Institute talked of tax policies that could help two parents.

In this book, we analyze the crisis in family law in the U.S., describe shared parenting in more detail, give the results of research on custody, and provide lots of other information about family life.

We hope this book will help children to get the better life that they deserve.

Shared parenting is no panacea. Life is full of problems. But we as a society must do what we can to preserve not only "the magic years"[1] of early childhood, but the joys of childhood for all children.

Introduction
How Can We Do it Better—
Divorce American-style

by
Vicki Lansky
Deephaven, Minnesota
"Practical Parenting" columnist for Sesame Street Parents' Guide
magazine, "Help" columnist for Family Circle *magazine, and the*
author of more than twenty books for parents of young children.
January 1993

Writing books for parents, I'm afraid, is not a guarantee for being a successful parent. I know. I've written over twenty books and, still, I've often felt inadequate to the job. Fortunately my two children have had the good grace to turn out to be lovely as well as achieving young adults.

They weathered the storm of divorce that their father and I subjected them to with no obvious ill effects, despite possible moments of "seasickness" as we first set sail on this sea of divorce. It's not because we always came up with the right response in each stage of our parenting history, but maybe it does have something to do with the fact that we really cared about our kids—even when we did it "wrong." We cared enough about them to know that kids need two parents. And to have a chance at being a good parent meant having each parent have access and significant time with each child. We cared enough about them to know that it was our job, even apart, to make them feel that their world was a pretty secure place. It was our job to let them know they were loved and that it was okay for them to love the other parent, even when we no longer loved each other. We cared enough about them not to put them into the battle lines either by arguing in front of them (though loud arguing was never our style) or making them privy to our differences on legal or financial points.

It probably was easier for them also because *they* were *not* the battle line of our divorce. We were able to focus that anger on figuring out an equitable split of our business and assets. It seems to me that most divorces have at least one major arena in which one or both try to "even" up the score—even if that only means going after what seems "fair" to one party. That can translate to money, a business, control of the divorce, the house, the dog—or the children. Yes, the children. Unfortunately, parents sometimes make their battle line their children. When they do, it spells pain, sorrow and grief—for the children.

My children have two homes. They talk and act like they have two homes. They seem to float quite comfortably between them. No, they did not feel this comfortable in the beginning. It took time. Nor was each year smooth or without its changes. And this is not how I envisioned a childhood for them. I had to put to rest my dream of a traditional family life for them and for me, as one of life's losses. It has certainly been different than the life that I envisioned; but, you know—it hasn't been bad. Sometimes putting the dream of our marriage and family life to rest is harder than the divorce itself. But, once we have done so, we can move forward with the emphasis on the more important and caring concerns that *do* make a difference—such as helping your ex-spouse be a parenting partner as you rearrange family life for your children.

The family, as we know it, may be changing with divorce but I believe you can still be a family. This takes acceptance of new ways of doing things when we divorce. I've seen shared parenting work successfully for others as well as myself. It takes work, reading, being open to new ideas, and tolerance when things don't go as planned. Our life style is certainly different from my family of origin, but my children have a strong family life.

We need all the help we can get to bring us together when we must live apart. The Children's Rights Council (CRC) is an association dedicated to that premise. Research has shown that *two parents* are in the best interest of their children. In this book, CRC shares information that speaks to this premise, some of which is known and much of which has not been widely disseminated. For professional and parent alike, this book is an important tool in knowing what our parenting options are and what they can be. I hope it will empower parents and the courts alike in our changing world.

Chapter 1

Children as Victims of Divorce

by
Elliott H. Diamond

The divorce industry

Speaking as the Chief Justice of the United States, Warren E. Burger stated that "The obligation of [the legal] profession is to serve as healers of human conflicts."[1] However, not all attorneys heed this advice.

Many attorneys encourage divorcing spouses to become enemies of each other and discourage spouses from using a conciliatory approach. The more heated the battle, the longer it will last and the more money the litigants will have to pay. "The modus operandi of lawyers, [is to] seek minor adjustments rather than comprehensive solutions; delay as much as they can; and frequently lay the groundwork for future conflict (which ensures future business for themselves)," states a George Washington University professor.[2]

Without practical consumer-oriented marriage laws and without mandatory requirements for mediation, victims of failing marriages are exploited nationwide. Victims are intimidated by legal jargon, required to appear in frightening courts, made to feel guilty about their failure as spouses, and then forced to pay large sums to their attorneys and possibly to their ex-spouse's attorney, as well.

In this manner, the adversarial form of divorce has become an industry that produces billions of dollars per year in income for attorneys.[3] Thus, the divorce industry diverts money that could have been spent on the children of failing marriages while further traumatizing spouses and their children.

To litigate or mediate?

Many people believe that the family-law court is the only means for divorcing spouses to resolve their disputes. Such disputes arise when issues such as child or spousal support, property distribution, child custody, or child access to his or her parents (visitation) cannot be resolved between the divorcing spouses.

But mediation, a form of dispute resolution, is an alternative to a grueling divorce war. Unfortunately it is neither encouraged nor made a first option by most judges or by most state laws. Its use, however, is growing. As of 1992, thirteen states had mediation statutes, up from seven states in 1980.[4]

When mediation is used, a couple is expected to spend at least three sessions with the mediator. If spouses and ex-spouses reach an amicable, out-of-court agreement with or without a mediator, they are required to petition the court for approval of their agreements. Although the court is always involved in the approval of divorce and related agreements, the legal costs are considerably less when agreements are reached before appearing in court.

Mediation has been proven to be effective, inexpensive, and less time-consuming and to eliminate much emotional trauma.[5] When divorcing spouses must resolve their disputes as adversaries, only the divorce industry wins.

Is our marital contract obsolete?

Another question in dealing with the issue of children and divorce takes a preventive approach. Can a better marital contract minimize disputes? We may get an answer to this question if we consider marriage a partnership and then look at other forms of partnership agreements.

When partnerships are formed for business purposes, it is a common practice to spell out the method for resolving disputes. Provisions for the dissolution of the partnership are also included. That is, business partners may agree on a mediator or arbitrator and on a method of dividing assets and liabilities in the event the business fails.

Partnership agreements are legal, encouraged by attorneys, and are upheld by our courts. In the event of a business failure, these agreements cause less anguish than if no such agreements existed. If disputes occur, or if the business fails, each partner is better prepared; they have already thought out and agreed to a solution.

However, in the case of marital contracts, the courts are slow to accept such an agreement.[6] Their reason is steeped in tradition and not in logic. The marriage ceremony originated as a religious function, performed by the church, and the contract was based upon an "until-death-do-us-part" commitment. There was no intention of breaking the contract and no need to plan for the demise of the marriage. However, in practice, marriage is often no longer a lifelong commitment, and, in view of the present high rate of divorce, such agreements may prove useful in avoiding litigation.

The courts currently believe that only they have the power to resolve marital disputes. They believe that divorce is promoted if spouses are permitted to spell out the terms of dissolution.[7] Because of this, pre-marital agreements that concern children, and sometimes property rights, will not always be considered legally binding.[8]

But the court's authority on these issues is slowly eroding as new state and federal laws help resolve marital disputes, whether or not these issues are addressed by a marriage contract. Will new laws permit future marriage contracts, like partnership agreements, to contain all the terms of dissolution?

A child's need for two parents, and the state's responsibility

Should a state deny children the love and care of a nurturing parent because the children's parents are divorced? That may well happen when joint custody is not considered a viable option by the courts or state legislatures.

Legal custody gives a parent the right to make decisions concerning the child's education, vacation, medical treatment, and religion. Physical custody relates to the child's residence. Living with a parent gives the child a close, loving, and personal relationship with that parent. Joint custody permits both parents to share the responsibilities and rewards of both legal and physical custody. A variety of joint-custody living arrangements are available which are suitable to the needs of minor children.

Forty-eight states now allow minor children of divorced parents the right to the love, guidance, and discipline of both parents through joint-custody laws (forty-three states) or court rulings.[9] (See Appendix B.) Despite joint-custody statutes and court rulings, customs are slow to change and many judges still favor mothers as the sole custodian.[10] In nineteen of the forty-three states which have joint custody laws, joint custody is the preference, unless it is not in the best interest of the child. In five other states, higher courts have said that joint custody may be awarded. This means that in forty-eight states either the legislature or higher courts favor joint custody as an option.

In the states with joint custody, ex-spouses can share in raising children. That is, each parent retains a portion of the legal and physical custody of the child through shared parenting. Thus, each spouse has the right to parent his or her child after divorce.

Thrust of new laws

The courts have begun to loosen their grip on settling all divorce disputes. For example, all fifty states have established community property or equitable property distribution laws that require an equal split of marital property,[11] thereby reducing the need for litigation.

Cases have also held that a spouse's pension fund is to be considered communal property.[12] Upon divorce, either pension payments are partitioned, or a lump-sum payment is awarded to the non-pensioned ex-spouse. In addition, the New York state high court ruled that a medical license received by a man whose wife helped put him through school has a long-term value that should be divided when the couple divorces.[13]

Federal guidelines and laws for enforcing child-support and spousal-support payments, with a minimum of court procedures, are being developed and implemented.[14] Additionally, laws regarding access of children to non-custodial parents, grandparents, and relatives are slowly evolving as state codes.

Through access enforcement and joint custody, children of divorce are permitted the love and guidance of all those who loved them prior to the divorce. Grandparents now have guaranteed access rights, by state law or court decisions, in 45 states. Stepparents are fighting for similar rights.[15]

A law establishing the venue for litigating child custody first became effective in 1968. The purpose of this law is to reduce child-snatching in parents' attempts to find another county or state more favorable to their cases.[16]

The pendulum of "favoritism" in divorce is swinging toward a more neutral position. Consider the issue of custody of minor children. Prior to 1910, women did not have the right to vote, few owned property, and job opportunities for women were scarce. Because women were without financial means and both women and children were considered as chattel of men, men were favored as the sole custodial parent.[17] However, from the 1920s through the 1960s mothers were favored as the sole custodial parent under the "tender years" doctrine.[18] Currently, more and more states are opting for the more neutral doctrine of joint custody.

The term "alimony" has been dropped by most states in favor of "spousal support," and it is now awarded, regardless of sex, on the basis of need rather than as a right.[19]

The thrust of changing divorce-related laws is to make ex-spouses self-supportive, independent, and equal with regard to equity in marital property and pensions. Likewise, the raising of children and paying their financial expenses are also headed in the direction of joint responsibility. However, all of the nation's legislators must be made aware of the thrust of these new laws and of the need in divorcing families for these equitable laws.

Two classes of children

A major objection to the recent trend in income redistribution is that it will create two classes of children: children of the first marriage make up one class, while children of a subsequent (and intact) marriage of the non-custodial parent make up the second class.

The children of a subsequent (intact) marriage can obtain economic benefits from a parent only if the parent is willing to provide them. No court can order the parent of an intact family to provide beyond the necessities. The parents of an intact marriage have the sole say as to how much they spend on their children. This is not so in the case of a dissolved marriage. The non-custodial parent has no vote on how his or her court-ordered child-support payments are spent.

Unlike children of a subsequent marriage, children of an earlier, dissolved marriage have a legal tie to their non-custodial parent's wallet. These children can go to court via the custodial parent to enforce their demands for more money, whereas the other class of children cannot.

The children of dissolved marriages (through the custodial parents) do not have to provide accountability as to how money is spent. Children of intact marriages do.

Is the establishment of two classes of children good for children? What effect will income redistribution have on second families? Are we dealing with a radical change in public policy which should be subject to public debate?

Access Denial?

Another central issue in post-divorce families is the denial of access for the non-custodial parent. Studies show that the custodial parent denies access or interferes with access in about 50 percent of the scheduled visits.[20] Denial of court-ordered access is a national epidemic, yet only a few states have addressed the child's need for enforced court-ordered access.

In the area of child-support enforcement, there are federal, state, and county agencies which work together to employ administrative and punitive means of enforcement. But few of our nation's county or state agencies will investigate access complaints. Fewer will order the custodial parent to allow for make-up of access denial. (At present, Michigan is the only state which both recognizes and attempts to remedy this problem.)[21]

Should state and local agencies that enforce child-support awards also enforce child-access awards? Should a judge's order for access deserve the same respect as an order for support? Would non-custodial parents have more respect for support orders if custodial parents had more respect for access orders?

A new look at marriage and dissolution

Prior to the advent of no-fault auto insurance, an American involved in an auto accident was in a situation of judicial crisis similar to that which many divorcing spouses now face. Without laws that spelled out the responsibilities of accident victims and insurance companies, these victims found that they had to use the court-devised adversary system to resolve their disputes. Many victims of auto accidents soon became victims of unscrupulous attorneys.

After much public and institutional outcry and effort of advocacy groups, most states enacted no-fault auto insurance laws. As a result, money from insurance claims went into the victims' pockets rather than to lawyers. Thus, reform was achieved and auto victims were not required to become adversaries in a protracted litigation process.

During the past twenty years, more and more contracts have become consumer-oriented; such contracts include lease agreements, purchase agreements, loans, and installment sales. State laws require that all provisions be clearly spelled out in large print and in non-legal, everyday terms. Also, the consumer has a right of recision within a specified time. Furthermore, state and county agencies are established to protect the consumer.

Should a one-month marriage require the same form of litigation as does a twenty-year marriage? Common sense says no, yet the courts say yes! Consumers have the automatic right to rescind other contracts within a specified period. Why not the right to rescind a marriage contract if spousal problems develop within six months and no children are born?

Upon dissolution of the marital contract, where children are born, federal, state and local agencies must protect children and families by establishment of administrative guidelines. At present, the federal government has empowered the Department of Health and Human Services to assist in the collection of financial child support.[22]

Similar assistance is needed to promote meaningful marriage contracts, child access ("visitation") enforcement, mediation, uniform and fair support orders, access to children's school records, joint custody, and many other divorce-related issues that affect children.

The divorced father: a pathetic image

Statistics show that the American father rarely gets custody of his minor children after divorce. Most state laws frustrate the male's attempt to gain custody.[23] As a result, many fathers perceive that the "system" is unjust, and they flee. Those who stay and cannot meet their child-support payments end up in court. Reports about irresponsible fathers who flee or cannot meet support payments often appear in the media;[24] they are portrayed as a disgrace to both their society and their children. This adverse publicity, with its concentration on delinquent fathers, leads many judges, as well as the public, to stereotype divorced fathers as uncaring.

But the image of the divorced American father is based upon media reports of a minority who deny their children financial support. Only an estimated 25 percent of fathers who are under child-support court orders do not comply in any manner with these orders.[25]

However, the media makes little mention of the 2.5 million divorced fathers who are financially responsible. They represent three times the number who pay nothing, and they pay an estimated 11.2 billion dollars in support annually.[26] These fathers love their children, go to great pains to visit them, and are grieved by the separation from their children. Some fathers are even emotionally disabled as a result of the separation.[27]

The typical American father is portrayed as "a Dagwood Bumstead, a well-meaning idiot who is constantly outwitted by his children, his wife and even his dog," states a Temple University professor.[28] After divorce, his image is further denigrated by the media.

By means of television, radio, and the printed word, the American father must be accurately portrayed; he is generally loving, caring, competent, protective, and financially responsible. This image must be projected across the nation in order that he gain the respect of his children, the courts, and the legislatures. Only by establishing this respect will the legislature and courts respond to the legal needs of the American father.

As one author states, "Maybe in time the men of the nation will tire of such emasculation and will let the offending parties know their feelings in no uncertain terms. Until it happens, though, the mass media's mass castration will proceed apace, and the contemporary American father will be ever more emphatically confirmed as a vestigial figure."[29]

Poverty and amorphous rage

Adversarial procedures often contribute to the instability of the troubled family.[30] Instead of a better life after divorce, this process can lead to a gradual decline into poverty and mental and psychological confusion for many divorcing families.

Of the millions of parents who consult with attorneys, many are encouraged to divorce their spouses. They are advised to seek a new life with unrealistic expectations of financial security and the possibility of a more compatible spouse or partner.[31]

Statistics show that married mothers who have become single-parent mothers have also become the fastest growing segment of the nation's new poor.[32] One must consider whether the feminization of poverty is linked to the feminization of custody.

As a result of unneeded and unwelcome divorce promoted by the divorce industry, millions of parents may have been unnecessarily separated from each other and from their children. Currently, more than 19 million children live in families where fathers are absent,[33] with divorce being a major cause for the father's absence. Possibly a less adversarial process could have found a solution to their ailing marriages other than divorce.

With the adversarial posture of divorce placing more and more children in the middle of custody battles, the prospect of losing custody in our courts or obtaining what are perceived as unfair custody determinations has motivated thousands of parents to snatch their children each year,[34] change names, and relocate.[35] Thus, the tragedy of divorce is compounded through sole-custody awards.

Millions of divorced women have discovered that they possess useless separation agreements. These agreements awarded them sole custody of minor children and promised financial security through court-ordered support payments. Ex-husbands with no custodial rights have vanished rather than pay, leaving mothers penniless and children fatherless.[36] On the other hand, fathers with court-awarded parental responsibility often "stay and pay."[37] It stands to reason that when the parents are around, so are their wallets.

Many people hope that new federal and state laws providing for wage assignment, liens, and federal and state tax intercepts will radically improve child support collections. But, however much support collections are improved, children need more than mere financial support.

There is a growing body of evidence that children, girls as well as boys, are psychologically and socially damaged in fatherless homes.[38] One study indicated that "in divorced families, contact with additional adult caretakers was associated with positive social behaviors shown by the child."[39]

Other studies showed that children, lacking a father's guidance, are unable to cope. Many never complete high school. Some children themselves become the parents of unwanted children. Some turn to drugs, some run away and are declared as "missing," and others turn to crime or suicide.[40] A professor of psychohistory states that "a vast army of sociopaths bred in fatherless homes and filled with boundless and amorphous rage for which they are not to blame will overrun this land."[41] This trend must be reversed. The father's role as a nurturing parent must be acknowledged by society and protected and encouraged by our courts.

Contempt for parents!

Sadly, contempt for parents is widespread in our society. Joan Berlin Kelly has noted that:

> When a father seeks a rich and continuing relationship with his children after divorce, male lawyers, judges and psychotherapists sometimes react with suspicion, derision or hostility. . .By having to go on the offensive to obtain a shared parenting arrangement, men frequently become cast into the role of troublemakers, when for many their intention is to continue a co-parenting role they established within the marriage family. When women oppose joint custody arrangements, they are less likely to be seen as trouble makers and their views less often challenged.[42]

Although there is a wealth of evidence that single fathers are competent at child-rearing,[43] many courts are reluctant to act on this evidence. The courts' refusals to allow fit fathers to continue to parent after divorce have caused many fathers to be angered by our justice system, depressed by the loss of a loved one, and distraught by the inability to share their lives with their children.

Examples of this bias against parents cover a wide range. For those fathers who prefer access instead of custody and are denied access by the custodial parent, the courts will rarely enforce an access agreement.[44] In addition, schools often frustrate the father's access to his child's school records.[45] Furthermore, the Federal Parent Locator Service (FPLS) will not assist the non-custodial parent in locating an ex-spouse in the event that the ex-spouse vanishes with a child; the FPLS is primarily used to locate non-custodial parents who owe support.

Fathers of low income families often "leave" their homes to enable their spouses to qualify for welfare payments as the head of a "fatherless" home. The family's total income is then increased by adding the welfare payment to the father's contribution.[46] By providing a financial incentive for a "fatherless" home, the government is discouraging responsible fatherhood.

Harsh treatment from the courts

Unlike other debts which may be litigated in civil courts, child support arises out of a court order. Thus, a father who is behind in his child support payment violates a court order, which is a criminal act, and is subject to imprisonment.[47] No other class of debtors, such as those owing consumer debts or owing Federal taxes, are so harshly treated.

Many of these fathers were unemployed and were unable to support their families during marriage. Now that they are divorced, some are harassed for being poor and are arrested as criminals.

The fact that many of these fathers are providing essential emotional support and non-material contributions for their children will not be considered by the courts as reason to diminish their prison sentences.

The fathers can provide little or no financial support once incarcerated, and the final effect of imprisonment may be merely to revoke from the child whatever emotional support the father offered. In addition to this, the child may be left with the stigma of having an incarcerated criminal for a parent.

All states have enacted laws that penalize the financially irresponsible parent, yet few states have laws that encourage fatherhood after divorce, that encourage fathers to make support payments,[48] that encourage fathers to visit and to raise their own children,[49] that penalize an ex-spouse who alleges child abuse in order to deny access or that credits divorced fathers with emotionally supportive contributions to their children.

In 1978, the right of a fit father to continue to parent after divorce was upheld as a constitutionally guaranteed right by the Supreme Court.[50] As a result of this decision and an increase in state joint-custody laws, more and more fathers realize that they do not have to give up their children upon divorce.

With an estimated 2.5 million fathers who pay billions of dollars yearly in child support, and with over 200 grass-roots divorce reform groups, fathers now have the clout to demand that the public and law-makers respect and encourage fatherhood as much as motherhood for the sake of our children.

From a mother's knot to a mother not: non-custodial mothers

Women, too, do not escape the punitive nature of our divorce system. Non-custodial mothers are especially subject to painful questioning and abuse.

About one-fourth of all American families with children are single-parent households. Fifteen percent of the single-parent households are headed by fathers. This means that an estimated 1.4 million fathers are heads of households.[51]

"What's wrong with you, mother, that you did not get custody?" is a question often asked of divorced mothers who do not have custody of their children. Society assumes that a mother without custody is unfit, and it often stigmatizes a woman whose knot with her children comes untied.

Not only does society pass a negative judgment, but the mother without custody often judges herself harshly for not retaining custody of her children.

Geoffrey Grief, Ph.D., an assistant professor of the University of Maryland School of Social Work and Community Planning, believes guilt to be "more pronounced" among non-custodial mothers than among non-custodial fathers. "It's clear that these [non-custodial] mothers' expectations of themselves and society's expectation of them are different than fathers. Fathers are expected to be fathers without custody."[52]

When one talks to non-custodial mothers, one often finds the same concerns that non-custodial fathers have: problems with lack of access to the children, difficulty in paying support, and the feeling of a loss of control.

Although fathers are being awarded sole custody in an increasing number of cases, should children of divorce be disassociated from their mothers?

Abuse of child-abuse laws

Unfortunately, many children are the victims of mental and physical abuse. They may be abused at home by parents or step-parents, and these deplorable situations must be ended. The neutral grounds of the school allow school personnel to identify an abused child. These children should be encouraged to articulate such experiences in this safe environment and steps should be taken to end the abuse.

But, compounding the tragedy of abuse, there are fathers who are denied custody or access rights by being falsely accused of child molestation.[53] A leading proponent of men's issues has observed that:

> It is difficult enough for fathers to gain equal access to child-rearing opportunities; the divorce process amounts to affirm-ative opposition by the government. Predictably, it is the children who are suffering far more from father deprivation than from father molestation.

Just as men fought to maintain dominance as workers, women are fighting to maintain dominance as parents. Accusations of child molesting have become one of their more effective weapons in this battle. It is important, then, not to allow a justifiable concern about abuse be exploited as a scare tactic by those who seek to maintain their monopoly of power over raising children.

There is a surprisingly fine line between molestation and healthy parent-child physical contact. Because of our sexist heritage, we tend to draw the line more narrowly for fathers than for mothers. A mother who playfully rubs her nose on her baby's tummy while changing a diaper would be considered to be an affectionate mother. A father who did so, however, could be accused of molestation by a hostile ex-wife and, barring a vigorous defense by the father, she could make those charges stick. Even with a vigorous and successful defense by the father, it could be a long time before his visitation rights were restored.[54]

Child abuse should not be tolerated, but neither should the abuse of child abuse laws.

Who pays?

The volume of divorce-related lawsuits increased rapidly during the 1970s and early 1980s, and the duration of these lawsuits is on the upswing.[55] The result is a backlog of cases, delays in litigation, and a lack of timely solutions.

Cases concerning the needs of children have become exceedingly complex, and their resolution often takes months and even years. Meanwhile, the child is growing while his or her needs have been put on hold by the court. Solutions, when finally adjudicated, are often either unexpected or inappropriate.

There are financial considerations as well as emotional costs to this backlog of divorce and custody fights, and many are hidden from all but the in-depth view. Not only does the victim of divorce pay his or her immediate legal costs, but both the victim and the public bear court costs and many hidden costs.

If the custodial parent's income is below the poverty level, taxes are increased to cover additional welfare and Aid to Families with Dependent Children (AFDC) payments.[56] More social workers, investigators, and administrators are also hired, and more government buildings are needed to house them, all at the taxpayers' expense.

When spouses divorce, especially as adversaries, the financial burden of raising their children is shifted, in full or in part, to the state, and hence to the taxpayer. Is it not time for taxpayers to realize they are paying for ineffective laws, an inefficient dispute resolution system, and the problems of children of divorce?

Implementing reform

In summary, divorce American-style is a game in which we all lose. A combination of outdated marital and divorce laws, contempt for parenthood, and the adversarial system result in the victimization of children through divorce, and the terrible costs to our families and our children mount at an alarming rate. It's time for broad-based and sweeping reform.

The public's image of the divorced American father and the legal concept of fatherhood must be improved. Parenthood must be encouraged in both intact and divorced families and must not end with divorce. A parent's image must be correctly portrayed as loving and caring, regardless of marital status. For the benefit of our children, parenthood must gain the respect of the courts and lawmakers.

Furthermore, the public must be made aware that children of divorce need a close relationship with both their fathers and their mothers in order to develop as socially responsible adults.

Our marriage contracts and related marital laws are obsolete. They do not permit prospective marriage partners to consider or to elect terms of dissolution. Prospective marriage partners are not prepared to handle many of the legal and litigious issues that arise from divorce, nor are they aware of an alternative to the adversarial system. Thus, when a marriage fails, issues of property, custody, and support are litigated as afterthoughts in a court of law, where spouses become adversaries.

If any industry turned out a product that had a 50-percent failure rate, as does the institution of marriage, then consumers would be alarmed and insist upon a government investigation and sweeping changes. Is not the American marriage in that condition today?

Researchers feel that "because [the rate of divorce is likely to increase], it is important that parents and children be realistically prepared for the problems associated with divorce that they may encounter. . .Divorce is one of the most serious crises in contemporary American life. It is a major social responsibility to develop support systems to aid the divorced family in coping with changes associated with divorce and in finding means of modifying or eliminating the deleterious aftereffects of divorce."[57]

The Children's Rights Council identified the following divorce-related areas that are in need of reform and believes that such reform will eliminate the deleterious aftereffects of divorce on children while helping to end the crisis in family law.

Laws Regarding	Objective of Reform
Dispute Resolution	Required mediation preferred to an adversarial forum
Child Support	Based on need and the reasonable cost of raising a child. Parents pay according to their ability, by formula, with credits for visitation.
Custody of Minor Children	Awarded jointly to both parents as a first preference if both parents are fit.
Visitation (Child Access)	Liberally granted to non-custodial parents, grandparents, and relatives. State or local enforcement with make-up of visitation denial.

Also, marital property and pensions should be equitably distributed, and marriage contracts should permit the terms of dissolution to be spelled out prior to marriage.

In addition to laws, an educational program is needed to inform the public on issues and responsibilities of marriage, parenting, and divorce. After all, shouldn't this educational process begin in our public schools rather than in our courts?

support is either not forthcoming or insufficient, the custodial parent must also fill the role of breadwinner/provider.

This is a crushing combination of expectations and burdens to place on the shoulders of one parent, and that one parent is often overwhelmed by the sheer enormity of the task. "Sole custody mothers have often reported that role strain and task overload are major problems. Increased demands of child care and outside work may stifle a divorced mother's social and recreational life, and the quality of her relationship with the children may ultimately suffer."[6]

Wallerstein and Kelly describe the "extraordinary stresses" a sole-custody parent experiences in an attempt to cope with "such matters as work, finance, household routine and child-care arrangements, distribution of household tasks, discipline, allocation of responsibility, and visiting arrangements."[7] The immediate results of this tremendous responsibility are "a pervasive feeling of high tension and hectic pressure."[8]

While the custodial parent is asked to be both parents to the child, the non-custodial parent suddenly finds that he or she is neither parent to the child. The non-custodial parent in the sole-custody arrangement is truly "on the outside looking in" with regard to his or her own child. He or she has no legal status to determine, and sometimes none even to influence, the present and future of the child. The non-custodial parent is reduced to the status of visitor, whose relatively short time with his child is now termed a "visitation." "The relationship between the visiting parent and the visited child has no counterpart, and therefore no model, within the intact family."[9]

If the non-custodial parent has a normal amount of access ("reasonable visitation" in the parlance of the courts) he will probably be able to see his children every other weekend, which adds up to four days per month, or forty-eight days per year, plus portions of some holidays.[10] If he is so fortunate as to have a pleasant, or at least tolerable, relationship with his former spouse, he may have much greater access opportunities. If he is not so fortunate, the custodial parent may obstruct his access to such an extent that he may not be able to interact with his child in any meaningful way at all.

The visitation parent is no longer a real parent to his or her child. The child no longer runs to him when hurt and no longer snuggles in his lap to watch television. He no longer puts his child to bed at night, and they no longer wake up together in the morning. They no longer share the simple, everyday meal together. These everyday, very ordinary interactions are the glue that bond parent to child and child to parent. Yet, the non-custodial parent is denied these things with his child. Only the parent with custody has the pleasure and the burden of real, ordinary, everyday interaction with the child. "A visiting relationship between parent and child is strange by its very nature. The daily events which structured the parent-child relationship have vanished. The roles are awkward and new, no longer defined by sharing meals or family tasks. Neither child nor parent fully shares the life of the other, nor is fully absent."[11]

Non-custodial parents react to these losses—the losses of status with the child, the loss of daily contact with the child, and the loss of intimacy with the child—in various ways, not all of which are constructive.

Some men, in particular, fall into a role that has been described as "Disneyland Daddy." These men attempt to substitute a whirlwind of events and activities with their child (all crammed into the short visitation period) for the simple, everyday trials and pleasures that were shared in the pre-divorce family. They wine and dine the child, rushing from this special event to that, and in so doing move further and further away from a normal parent-child relationship with the child. They become caricatures of parents. The visitation parent is on the periphery of the child's everyday life. He or she is no longer a father or mother, but rather a "bearer of gifts and taker to circuses."[12] The relationship with the child becomes one of roles without content.

> Periodic visitation with a non-custodial parent is a notoriously unsatisfactory experience for all parties, which leads to eventual estrangement. The relationship with Sunday afternoon Daddy, "all pizza and no homework," is artificial at best. Over time it fades to no relationship at all, as the non-custodial parent withdraws from the artifice and guilt of the visitation routine.[13]

The Disneyland Daddy role has its roots in the guilt many parents (both mothers and fathers) feel toward the divorce and in the desperation of many non-custodial parents to preserve some sort of meaningful relationship with their children.

It is often those parents with the greatest emotional and psychological attachments to their children who find the entire experience of visitation too painful. Many eventually cease to visit their children at all.

> Men who were depressed following the divorce found it painful to visit their children. Often they visited irregularly or not at all.
>
> Fathers rejected by wives who had sought the divorce often expected to be rejected by their children as well. They were preoccupied with their own shame, grief, and lowered self-esteem. Some were preoccupied with their expendability in the

family system and talked bitterly about how little they were needed, how quickly they would be replaced by 'male role models,' by the new lover or stepfather.[14]

This psychological withdrawal and accompanying lack of visitation on the part of the non-custodial parent can, of course, have a very disturbing and damaging effect on the child, who does not understand why his father (or mother) no longer even comes to visit. This process can—and often does—heighten the child's feelings of abandonment, loss, insecurity, guilt, and lowered self-esteem. Wallerstein and Kelly found that "...the children...were profoundly disappointed when the expected father did not arrive. They were hurt and angry, and sometimes pretended that they didn't really care. Tragically, the fathers who were most likely to be depressed following the divorce were those who most loved or needed their children to restore their own faltering self-esteem. Yet, the children were rarely able to appreciate the root cause of the father's inconstancy and they experienced his not coming as confirming his lack of interest in them."[15]

Thus, one can see how the poor post-divorce adjustment of the non-custodial parent profoundly affects the adjustment of the children. The parents and children in the system of sole custody, or any other system of custody, are not independent players, but rather dependent partners in the post-divorce adjustment of themselves and their children. Whatever detracts from the psychological adjustment of either of the parents has its effect on the other parent, and on the children as well. The sole-custody arrangement certainly detracts from the adjustment of the non-custodial parent by removing him or her from the life of the child and by removing the child from his or her life. As has been frequently shown, this often leads to the withdrawal of the non-custodial parent, with serious effects on the children and, therefore, the custodial parent.

The child in sole custody

Research demonstrates conclusively that children suffer psychologically when their parents divorce or separate. While some psychological pain is inherent in the divorce experience itself, much of the psychological trauma for the child stems directly from the sole-custody/visitation system. Since sole custody is far more frequently granted to mothers than to fathers, most studies have necessarily focused on the mother in the role of custodial parent and the father in the role of visiting parent.

In describing and interpreting the psychological reactions of children to the divorce of their parents, and the sole-custody/visitation arrangement which accompanied that event, we will quote extensively from the observations of Drs. Judith Wallerstein and Joan Kelly in their seminal study of children in divorcing households, *Surviving the Breakup.*[16]

Drs. Wallerstein and Kelly conducted a longitudinal (five-year) study of 60 families containing 136 children (131 of whom participated in the study) for the California Children of Divorce Project from 1971 to 1977. This represents, without question, the most in-depth, comprehensive psychological study of the effects of divorce and post-divorce family adjustments on children and adults that has been undertaken.

Wallerstein and Kelly divided the sample of children, in response to the varying data, into four sub-groups:

* 2- to 5-year-olds
* 6- to 8-year-olds
* 9- to 12-year-olds
* 13- to 18-year-olds

Children in sole custody react very strongly and very negatively to the absence of the non-custodial parent. This reaction is the predominant observable psychological characteristic of the child in sole custody. "All of the research on divorce has suggested that the loss of a continuing parent-child relationship is the single most critical variable in the adjustment of the child."[17]

In describing the psychological reactions of children to their parents' separation and eventual divorce, Wallerstein and Kelly found these responses, among others:

1. fear
2. regression
3. bewilderment
4. denial
5. increases in aggressive behavior
6. inhibition of aggressive behavior
7. guilt
8. grief and mourning
9. feelings of deprivation
10. yearning for the departed parent
11. anger[18]

Some of the observations of Drs. Wallerstein and Kelly concerning the psychological disturbances felt by the children following the "loss" of one parent through the divorce/sole-custody system follow:

Children expressed the wish for increased contact with their fathers with a startling and moving intensity. An average of five months after separation, in our study, two-thirds of the youngsters were seeing their fathers at least twice a month. Their visits were, thus, at a level deemed "reasonable," yet there was great dissatisfaction.[19]

The most striking response among the 6- to 8-year-old children was their pervasive sadness. The impact of separation appeared to be so strong that the children's usual defenses and coping strategies did not hold sufficiently under the stress. Crying and sobbing were not uncommon, especially among the boys, and many children were on the brink of tears as they spoke with us.[20]

This profound feeling of loss was common in children of all age groups in the study:

It seemed clear to us in confronting the despair and sadness of these children and their intense, almost physical, longing for the father, that inner psychological needs of great power and intensity were being expressed.[21]

Particularly striking in [the 6- to 8-year-old] age group was the yearning for the father. More than half of these children missed their father acutely. Many felt abandoned and rejected by him and expressed their longing in ways reminiscent of grief for a dead parent. While it is not surprising that most children missed their fathers, the intensity of the response in this age group, especially among the boys, was notable and again, it had no relation to the degree of closeness between the father and child during marriage.[22]

Even the adolescents, the oldest age group and the most mature psychologically, were not immune. "These adolescents experienced a profound sense of loss. Some reacted with profound grief, as if they had lost a beloved person. They reported feelings of emptiness, tearfulness, difficulty in concentrating, chronic fatigue, and very troublesome dreams."[23]

These reactions were observable in the children for the life of the study:

Aside from pleas to reunite their parents, the most pressing demand children brought to counseling was for more visiting. The intense longing for greater contact persisted undiminished over many years, long after the divorce was accepted as an unalterable fact of life.[24]

Clearly, with single-parent custody, the preservation of the child's relationship with the non-custodial parent is in jeopardy. The frequency of children's contact with non-custodial fathers decreases rapidly over time and does so especially for daughters.[25]

Furthermore, in sole custody, the child eventually becomes more and more isolated from the non-custodial parent's entire family (kinship) system. Grandparents, particularly, often find it difficult or impossible to continue a relationship with the grandchild once that child is in the sole custody of one parent. Some grandparents have been forced to seek relief from the courts in their quest for continuing access to the grandchild following the divorce of the parents.

Several studies have shown that non-custodial fathers visit less frequently over time—and there is some evidence that children's contact with the kin of the non-custodial father is directly proportional to the frequency of his visits. These studies suggest that single-parent custody may eventually truncate one-half of the child's kinship network.[26]

Many studies, spanning years of psychological research, have documented various negative effects of "father absence" on the psychosocial development of children. These effects have been observed most frequently in boys.[27] Relatively few studies have been done on the consequences of "mother absence," however, possibly reflecting the infrequency of sole-father custody.

One consistent finding of divorce research is that adjustment problems are more intense and persistent for boys than for girls. The greater problems that boys experience after divorce may be a function of custody policy that has awarded them more often to their mothers.[28]

The sole-custody/visitation arrangement is also detrimental in other ways. Economically speaking, the single-parent, female-headed household suffers a grossly disproportionate incidence of poverty in American society. Yet, this is exactly the household engendered by sole custody. Thus, in the system of sole custody, the economic unit charged with the care of dependents is that one which has the least economic resources available to do so. The non-custodial parent's resources are frequently unavailable to the custodial parent in sole custody.

Sole custody, along with the adversarial courtroom process, often serves to drive a wide wedge of hostility between the divorcing parents.

"In sole custody arrangements one parent is placed in a position of authority over the other, which is bound to produce resentment. The fact that the non-custodial parent's opportunities to be with the children are reduced often creates conflict—much to the children's detriment."[29]

The non-custodial parent finds him- or herself at the center of a contradiction. While he or she is discouraged from being a real parent to the child in sole custody, he or she is, on the other hand, financially responsible for the child. "A visiting father in a sole custody arrangement is likely to resent the fact that while he may be the primary (if not total) child-support contributor, his access to the children is significantly restricted."[30]

The non-custodial parent, along with his or her extended family, is a critical source of support for both the custodial parent and the child. To the extent that the sole-custody/visitation system discourages the parents from cooperating, and instead encourages conflict, the system is detrimental to all concerned.

One study found that a continued positive relationship with the ex-husband was the most salient informal support system relating to the custodial mother's effectiveness in dealing with her children.[31]

The loosening of psychological bonds between the non-custodial parent and the child, much of which is the direct consequence of the sole-custody/visitation system, is probably a significant factor in the documented lack of compliance with court orders for child-support payments. Thus, sole custody may be potentially detrimental economically as well as psychologically.

Joint custody as an alternative

Joint physical custody is a viable option. It is possible for parents to separate their intimate spousal relationship from their parenting relationship, to build on the residue of respect of one another, and to develop a cooperative, civilized relationship for child rearing.[32]

Joint custody is more than a viable option. Joint custody is a preferable alternative to sole custody. What, exactly, is meant by the term "joint custody?"

Joint custody is many things; it is an ideal, a policy, and a set of expectations that influences how parents and children live and relate to one another after marital separation. The following ideas and values distinguish joint custody: first, both parents are viewed as equally important in the psychological and physical life of the child; second, both parents share authority for making decisions about the children; third, parents cooperate in sharing the authority for and the responsibilities in raising their children; and fourth, children spend a significant amount of time living with each parent.[33]

When I use the term "joint custody," I envision a custodial arrangement that attempts to approximate as closely as possible the flexibility in the original two-parent home. In such an arrangement, both parents have equal rights and responsibilities for their children's upbringing, and neither party's rights are superior. There is no structured visitation schedule. The children live in both homes. They do not live in one house and visit the other.[34]

Alternately,

. . .joint custody is not defined as an equal 50/50 sharing of the child's time, although it may include that, but rather a post-divorce parenting plan which goes beyond traditional visitation to include each parent at least 30 percent of the time, or more, in the child's ongoing life.[35]

As one can see from the above excerpts, the concept of joint custody stems from several premises. First, joint custody assumes that it is in the child's—"as well as the parents'"—best interest to have the active, shared involvement and support of two parents. Joint custody arrangements encourage both parents to invest time, money, and love into their relationship with their child by making it possible for each parent to spend significant amounts of time with the child.

In joint custody, neither parent is a "visitation parent." Neither parent is structurally "locked out" of the child's life. Thus, in joint custody one parent is not in a superior position of authority or decision-making power with regard to the other parent. Joint custody more closely approximates the equity of authority between parents that ordinarily exists in marriage. In joint custody neither parent is in a position to unilaterally impose his or her will on the other parent with regard to the child.

Joint custody encourages cooperation between the parents. Neither parent dominates the other. Neither parent dictates to the other. The facilitated cooperation between parents can only be of benefit to the child. Joint custody is conciliatory; it is not adversarial.

Joint custody recognizes that, if at all possible, the parents should always decide the best arrangements for themselves and their child. In so doing, joint custody recognizes the autonomy of the family—even the divorcing family. In joint custody, therefore, there are more negotiated arrangements and fewer imposed settlements. The value of this is reflected in the fact that studies have shown that joint-custody judgments result in approximately half the rate of relitigation of sole-custody judgments.[36]

This is obviously beneficial to society, to parents, and to children. Family courts are struggling under a heavy case load. Custody and support cases account for a large percentage of all family court cases. When reciprocal support cases are added in, the percentage of family court cases directly related to issues of custody and/or support becomes even greater.

The court system is being overwhelmed by its case load. To the extent that joint custody fosters conciliation or mediation, instead of litigation, and to the extent that joint custody results in lower rates of relitigation, it serves to ease the burden on the court system, with a concomitant savings in court expenses for the general public.

However, joint custody's greatest advantage is to the child. In joint custody the child is spared the most devastating psychological disruption that accompanies the divorce experience—the loss of a continuing involvement with the non-custodial parent. As the psychological literature previously cited clearly illustrates, it is the loss of the child's relationship with the non-custodial parent that is the chief cause of the grief, sorrow, anger, and depression so common to children of divorced parents.

Joint custody recognizes that, for the child, neither parent is "disposable" and neither parent can be treated as such. Joint custody recognizes that while there may or may not be a "primary caretaker," most children have two "psychological parents" and they are of equal value to the child.

Joint custody is also a more positive arrangement economically than is sole custody. Studies have found that in joint custody, as opposed to sole custody, parents charged with the primary financial support of the child make both higher levels of payment and more consistent rates of payment.[37] It is certainly more likely that a parent would financially support a child with whom he or she spends considerable, active parenting time than a child whom he or she merely visits once or twice a month. And certainly it seems logical to assume that a parent will positively support a child when they are actually living together. Both of these conditions are encouraged in joint custody.

The artificial separation of the monetary aspects of child rearing from the daily care and nurturing aspects of child rearing, and the isolation of the child with one parent to the exclusion of the other parent, lead to the lack of voluntary compliance with court-ordered child-support arrangements that is so problematic across the country. This is a major weakness of the sole-custody/visitation system. Joint custody seeks to share both the burdens and the joys of child rearing more equitably between the parents than does sole custody.

With joint custody, grandparents and other members of the extended family will have a greater probability of maintaining contact with the child after the divorce of the parents. The continued and enhanced involvement of the non-custodial parent will lead to the continued availability of his or her family system. They will be able to lend support to the divorcing family when it is most seriously in need of support.

Joint custody may also aid in lowering the incidence of one of the nation's most serious child-related social problems—child abuse. A study conducted by The American Humane Association, an independent, non-profit organization in Denver which reported on abuse statistics until the mid-1980s, found that 48 percent of all reported child-abuse cases occurred in single-caretaker homes for the year 1982. By making available to the single parent a larger network of support (social, psychological, and financial), joint custody will lessen the stress and pressure inherent in single, sole-custody parenthood.

Joint custody will also be of benefit to those parents (mostly mothers) who are now sole-custodial parents. These parents will enjoy a greater personal freedom when they no longer need to entirely bear the obligation to care for the child. For women, in particular, this greater freedom can translate into a better employability and a greater ability to compete in the job market. Women who no longer have to be the sole custodian of children will be able to do other things; they can finish school, begin college, and increase their job-related skills. Child care will be less of an obstacle when child rearing is more equitably shared among both parents and their respective families.

The work of anthropologist Carol Stack (Duke University), which focuses on the poorer and working class black community, indicates that some forms of "multiple custody" play a large role in the care of children in those communities. She found that the kinship networks of both parents are an essential resource, whether or not the parents ever actually marry.[38]

As previously noted, joint custody shares the burden of child care and support. In these poorer communities, multiple-custody modes of child rearing are an adaptation to the pressures of raising children with meager and insufficient economic resources. For these parents, joint-custody legislation will serve to give legal sanction to modes of social behavior already well-established and highly functional.

Joint custody is clearly a superior arrangement for the majority of divorcing families—and particularly for their children. Joint custody arrangements have been thoroughly studied by many mental-health professionals, sociologists and psychologists. Their conclusions have generally been very positive, and often they have been glowingly positive. "From a psychological point of view, joint custody is probably the healthiest and most desirable of the various custody plans available to divorced parents and their children."[39]

Joint custody offers both parents the opportunity and the challenge of continuing an active and positive parenting role after separation or divorce. This is to the benefit of both the child and the parents. Fathers, in particular, find that in joint custody they are able to continue to be a real parent to their child. "A different quality of psychological involvement grows out of the opportunity to take care of (i.e., to be a parent to) one's child, rather than "visit" with one's child. Fathers with joint custody are more likely to involve themselves in all aspects of their child's growth and development. The maintenance of such ties can be critical for both father and child."[40]

By encouraging positive interaction and cooperation between parents, as opposed to the warfare that so often characterizes custody resolution in the sole-custody system, joint custody is of benefit to both parents.

> The overriding benefit for these [joint custody] parents was the sharing of the burdens and pleasures of child rearing. Most of the working mothers valued time off to pursue their careers and their adult social life. Their sense of identity and self-esteem, gained from their paid employment, allowed them more easily to relinquish the role of full-time parent. For fathers, the preservation of a close relationship with their children and an important adult role as a parent was paramount. For these parents, shared parenting helped temper the sense of loss, personal failure, and disruption of the adult role and identity that often accompanies divorce. It functioned as an antidote to the diminished sense of self-esteem and guilt over breaking up the family. It allowed them to preserve a sense of family and to avoid the profound sense of loss for themselves and their children. The marital relationship had failed, but joint custody represented a personal and mutual success as parents.[41]

Primarily, however, the focus must and should be on the child. Joint custody has been found, with few exceptions, to be a good arrangement for the children of divorcing or separating parents. In joint custody, the child does not lose either parent, which is the critically negative factor in sole custody.

> Joint custody was beneficial for these children in three major areas. First, they received the clear message that they were

loved and wanted by both parents. Second, they had a sense of importance in their family and the knowledge that their parents made great efforts to jointly care for them, both factors being important to their self-esteem. Third, they had physical access to both parents, and the psychological permission to love and be with both parents.[42]

The strength of joint custody lies in its recognition of one simple fact: two parents are better than one. A child is born to two parents, and joint custody seeks to encourage both of those parents to be real parents to their child.

Society is at a loss when loving, caring, committed parents are systematically denied the means of constructive input into the lives of their own children. The increasing incidence of social ills that affect the young—teenage pregnancy, drug and alcohol abuse, teenage suicide, increasingly violent youth crime, high drop-out rates—all speak to the declining ability of the family to ameliorate the negative influences of the larger society upon youth. Under such circumstances, can we afford to unnecessarily weaken the family by excluding one parent? Can we afford to throw away even one resource that is available?

We should do everything in our power to maximize contact between the child and both parents. One clear way of doing that is through joint custody arrangements.[43]

Children need their fathers and their mothers. Children have need of, and the right to, two parents. This society can no longer afford to treat one of those parents as "disposable."

At its best, joint custody: (i) is flexible; (ii) recognizes the individuality of children and families; (iii) recognizes that the enduring and tenacious nature of parent-child attachment does not go away with divorce; (iv) calls forth a strength and maturity on the part of parents in order to put their children first at a time of personal debilitation; (v) acknowledges the original family as a valuable structure for child rearing, even though the marriage has been dissolved; and (vi) addresses the reality of changes in society and the family.[44]

Joint custody is not magic. It is not a panacea for the web of social problems affecting children in modern society. It is a means for increasing parental involvement in the lives of their children. Joint custody is a positive step toward the strengthening of the post-divorce family.

Divorce is a fact of modern American life. Joint custody can help make that reality a little less painful for the children and parents of divorcing families.

Joint custody (shared parenting) as a fundamental right

[Some legal scholars believe that joint custody is a constitutional right. The Children's Rights Council subscribes to this view. Holly Robinson, in the article "Joint Custody: Constitutional Imperatives," *The University of Cincinnati Law Review*, Vol. 54, No. 1 (1985) agrees. The following fifteen paragraphs are reprinted directly from her article. For more information, you may wish to refer directly to her article.]

The family, one of society's most fundamental institutions, increasingly has been subjected to breakdown, fragmentation and restructuring. Breakdowns that occur in families containing children often present courts with the difficult task of determining which parent should receive custody of the children.[45] Many jurisdictions, by statute, give threshold recognition to the principle that, in the absence of misconduct, both parents have an equal right to the custody of their children. Traditionally, however, courts have viewed the right to custody as one belonging exclusively to the "victor" of a contested custody proceeding. Thus, a judge presiding over a custody matter typically will feel compelled to make a choice between the parents involved. In making such a choice, judicial concerns regarding the protection of parental equality generally are replaced by the desire to protect the right of the "deserving" parent.

In order to give real substance to the concept that each parent has an equal right to custody, custody awards should, as a matter of law, be granted jointly, unless there are compelling reasons why an exclusive award is required to serve the child's interests. Ideally, whether inside or outside the context of marriage, parenting is a shared responsibility undertaken by both parents. Custody awards should reflect this ideal where feasible.

Joint custody[46] has been proposed as the preferred alternative to exclusive custody on a number of policy grounds.[47] A few states have adopted, either by legislative or judicial action, joint custody as the presumptively proper custody arrangement,[48] and several other states have authorized joint custody as an option to be considered by the courts making custody awards.[49] In addition, a number of commentators[50] have argued in favor of greater use and encouragement of joint custody by state courts, although these efforts largely have been limited to policy arguments and proposals for statutory interpretation.

This article seeks to shift the joint custody debate to an entirely different plane: it argues that current constitutional doctrine, when applied to the parent-child relationship, mandates a presumption on the part of states that joint custody is the proper means of giving appropriate recognition to each parent's fundamental right to be intimately involved in the upbringing of his or her child. The article recognizes that exclusive custody is permissible, but suggests that this is so only in circumstances where the child would clearly be harmed by a joint custody arrangement. This article also suggests that the "best interests of the child" standard, as it traditionally has been articulated and applied, does not justify denial to either parent of a share in custodial rights and responsibilities.

In order to develop these points, the article first outlines the concept of joint custody and reviews briefly the advantages and disadvantages of exclusive custody. Second, the article addresses the limited reception joint custody has had in American law.

The concept of joint custody

"Joint custody" as a legal concept emerged from a dissatisfaction with the consequences of the concept of sole custody.[51] Sole custody and the adversarial process that generates it result in serious problems for both the parents and children involved. For the parents, the "winner take all" consequences of the traditional emphasis on exclusive custody awards typically fuel the bitter intense frictions already existing as a result of a deteriorated marriage. For children, the transfer of parental hostilities from the home to the courtroom merely represents a continuation, if not an intensification, of a painful situation that they see themselves as virtually helpless to influence.

During an intact marriage, both parents legally are vested with equal authority to make decisions concerning their child and they must cooperate in reaching those decisions.[52] Divorce terminates the marriage but not the family; therefore, while the parties to the marriage no longer occupy the roles of husband and wife with regard to each other, they retain the roles of father and mother in relation to the children of the marriage. Because the same parent-child relationships continue to exist after parents separate, the rights and responsibilities of both parents toward their children logically should remain the same as prior to separation, unless special reasons dictate otherwise.

Under current practice, however, the formerly equal and joint decision-making authority of the parents is typically replaced by a grant of exclusive decision-making authority to one parent, and a denial of virtually all such authority to the other.[53] Modern research has revealed the severely adverse consequences of this approach. The physical, emotional, and psychological problems often experienced by children and parents after divorce formerly were thought to result from the inherently traumatic nature of the divorce process itself. However, recent scientific evidence now has linked several of these problems directly to two phenomena that often accompany one another: parental conflict and the sole-custody arrangement.[54]

It has been argued that the present approach to custody determination should be changed. Both the adversarial system of custody adjudication and the sole-custody model encourage an all-or-nothing battle rather than cooperation between the parents. Both require the courts to select a winner (custodial parent) and a loser (non-custodial parent). The alternative of joint custody has been put forth as the model that reflects a commitment to continuing the equal rights and responsibilities and shared, cooperative parenting that existed during the marriage.[55] By requiring the parents to share decision-making and caretaking responsibilities regarding the child, joint custody maximizes the child's physical and emotional access to both parents in meaningful, day-to day interaction, and helps the child to see both parents as sources of love and security and as positive role models.[56]

By relieving some of the stresses inherent either in full-time parenting or in the complete lack of involvement in parenting,[57] joint custody also can have positive psychological and practical effects on parents, which in turn can enhance the relationships between the child and each parent.[58] In fact, it has been argued that, by requiring parents to share the responsibility for decision-making, joint custody actually may help to minimize the need for power struggles between parents.[59] The joint-custody model thus may provide the most effective method of implementing the states' paramount public policy interest—the protection of the best interests of the children of divorced parents.

Several arguments have been leveled at joint custody, however. One argument is that joint custody increases the potential for parental conflict by requiring continued interaction between persons who have divorced. This argument misses the point, however, in that the problem of parental conflict exists regardless of the type of custody arrangement that has been instituted. It is the existence of the child and not the imposition of a particular custody decree that makes continued contact between divorced parents necessary.[60] There is some evidence that the level of parental conflict is no greater and may even be less in a joint-custody arrangement than it would be in a sole-custody arrangement.[61]

A second and more serious argument against joint custody simply is that the parents will refuse to cooperate. Several factors must be argued in response to this concern. First, the increasing number of parents across the country voluntarily seeking joint custody arrangement indicates that many parents in fact desire the opportunity to cooperate in child rearing after divorce. Second, even in situations where the parents are totally unable to subordinate their personal animosities to their concern for the welfare of their children, it is not necessarily true that sole custody would be more appropriate than joint custody. It is extremely questionable whether warring parents could cooperate with any greater success in an arrangement involving limited access than one where custody is split more evenly. The need for positive interaction between the parents and the need for each parent to strive to preserve the child's positive image of the other parent exists in a sole custody arrangement as it does in a joint custody arrangement.

Regardless of the form of the custody decree, children can be expected to suffer damaging effects from parental conflict and also from the extended absence or non-availability of one parent.[62] No custody arrangement can guarantee protection against the former, but joint custody at least prevents the latter. In fact, non-custodial parents easily could argue that it is precisely in the "hostile parent" situation that they are most in need of the legal protection afforded by joint custody.[63] This is because a hostile custodian may prevent the non-custodial parent from having access to the children.

Further, parents who allow their own personal animosities to override their concern for their child's welfare and healthy development are not acting to protect their child's best interests. Although hostility and even conflict may be inevitable, it is not inevitable that the conflicts create difficulties for the child. It not only is possible but necessary for mature adults to separate their feelings toward each other from their functioning as parents.[64]

Children have enough difficulty adjusting to the necessary restructuring of their physical and emotional environment that follows a divorce without having to cope with being a battlefield for their parents' hostility. It may be argued that parents should be required to accept the consequences naturally flowing from their behavior, and that the state should make it clear to them that failure adequately to discharge parental responsibilities may result in a forfeiture of parental rights. [This is the end of excerpts from Holly Robinson's article.]

Dissatisfaction with a system that favors sole custody has prompted the argument that joint custody (shared parenting) is a desirable alternative to the traditional approach. The following points in favor of joint custody have evolved through give-and-take in testimony before legislators in several states. They are based for the most part on studies published between 1978 and 1990. Appendix A summarizes many of these studies published as journal articles or available as doctoral dissertations. It is obvious from these studies that there are many benefits for the children of joint custody that are not available to their sole-custody counterparts.

Rapid-Fire Points In Favor of Joint Custody (Shared Parenting)

1. Practice for hundreds of years in Roman, English and U.S. law was that father had custody. Since about 1920, presumption has switched to mothers. Best interest of the child is almost automatically interpreted as sole custody and the sole custodian is the mother, according to U.S. Census Bureau figures released in 1992. Yet it seems that most children want to live with both parents whether or not their parents are divorced. Joint custody enables them to do so.

2. The past twenty-five years have seen a tripling of the divorce rate in the U.S. Nationally, more than one million children are affected each year by the divorce of their parents. Joint physical custody will enable these children to have the love and care of both parents after divorce, alleviating many of the problems associated with sole custody.

3. Joint custody is the fastest-growing concept in 20th-century family law. In 1980, it was accepted in three states. Now, it is accepted in forty-eight states and the District of Columbia, indicating that legislators from around the country understand children's need for close and continuing contact with both parents after divorce.

4. In nineteen of those states, joint custody or shared parenting is the presumption or preference. In twenty-four states, joint custody is an option. In five additional states, higher courts of the state have said judges may give joint custody. Only one state, South Carolina, does not permit joint custody. The North Dakota statute is silent about joint custody. The nineteen states with a presumption or preference are California, Connecticut, Florida, Idaho, Iowa, Kansas, Louisiana, Maine, Michigan, Minnesota, Mississippi, Missouri, Montana, Nevada, New Hampshire, New Mexico, Oklahoma, Oregon, and Utah. The preference and presumption laws send a message to parents that both are important to children and should stay involved in their children's lives after divorce. *But note that in some of those states joint custody is a presumption or preference only if both parents agree.* See Appendix B for information about the status of joint custody in all the states.

5. Studies of children of divorce agree that mutual respect between

the parents is a key factor in determining how the children will fare in the post-divorce family. The adversarial system in the courts is a system which serves to destroy that variable of respect, rather than reinforcing it as joint custody does. No system is a panacea for life's problems, but, in general, joint custody encourages cooperation.

6. The courts must consider the best interest of the child, but most people agree that the court system as a forum for settling custody disputes is contrary to the best interests of the child.

7. Warren Burger, the former Chief Justice of the United States, urged attorneys to be "healers." Healing can occur by providing incentives for cooperation, rather than by encouraging litigation.

8. There are about 100,000 custody battles in the U.S. each year. This is about 10 percent of all divorcing couples. These battles cost millions of dollars that would be better spent on the children and the families. Much emotional trauma is also expended on such battles, in which children are the primary victims as they are pulled between parents. A presumption for joint custody can help cut down on custody battles.

9. The Census Bureau reported in 1992 that 15 percent of single-parent homes are headed by men—the fastest growing custody group in the country. Although this is a statistically small group, Mothers Without Custody (MW/OC), a national organization, notes that numerically it represents 2,000,000 non-custodial mothers. Non-custodial mothers have the same problems as non-custodial fathers. They want to be more involved in their children's lives.

10. Non-custodial fathers and non-custodial mothers are reduced to occasional visitors in their own children's lives. Extended kin, including grandparents, especially if they are on the non-custodial parent's side of the family, also have greater difficulty in obtaining access. . .because their rights flow from those of the non-custodial parent. Joint custody ensures access of the child to the extended family.

11. Joint custody is both legal and physical. Legally, it means shared decision-making on the major decisions affecting the child, such as education, medical matters, religion, and area of residence. As in marriage, these decisions may be allocated between parents. Physically, it means the time spent should be as nearly equal as possible with each parent, though not necessarily a 50-50 split. Generally, it means at least a third of the time with the child by a parent on a year-round basis, with

a variety of arrangements possible to suit the needs of the restructured family of divorce. It is joint physical custody that is important to children. Visitation generally means only about 15-18 percent of the time on a year-round basis with the child.

12. Although joint custody is partly an outgrowth of the feminist and women's movement (urban anthropologist Carol Stack popularized the phrase "joint custody" in 1976), some feminists are wary of joint custody. They feel it would affect women's control over children and financial child support. However, joint custody provides time for women to pursue job, education, or career opportunities.

13. Seeing your children is not the same thing as parenting them. The term "visitation" is not used in joint custody decrees. Instead, the terms "be with" or "reside with" are used; with joint custody, one is considered to be a "parent," not just a "visitor" in the child's life.

14. A presumption or preference means joint custody should be given in most cases, unless there is a good reason not to give joint custody. If neither parent wants joint custody, or if there is proven abuse, the presumption can be overcome. If one parent wants joint custody, however, the other parent should not be able to defeat joint custody without sufficient reason.

15. Presumption for joint custody offers the benefit of the doubt to parents. It sends the message that both children and parents would benefit from joint custody and the parents have the best interests of the children at heart, unlike sole custody, which is a blueprint for an adversarial relationship that falls prey to attorneys and to the court.

16. A mere option for joint custody is insufficient because it does not send a strong enough message to parents and judges that shared parenting is in the best interest of children. In Nevada, where an option bill was created by the legislature, it was found in two years that only one family had been given joint custody, in a case where husband and wife lived only a few blocks from each other. The woman legislator who had introduced the original option bill became a co-sponsor of the a bill to upgrade the option to presumption, and it passed.

17. The Census Bureau reported in 1992 that 90.2 percent of parents with joint custody paid their child support, 79.1 percent of parents with access paid their child support, and only 44.5 percent of parents with neither joint custody nor access paid their child support. The Census

Bureau also reported that 7 percent of fathers had joint custody, 55 percent of fathers had access, and 38 percent of fathers had neither joint custody nor access.

18. Although proven abuse can serve to rebut the presumption, state judges' associations and state conciliation court systems with which we are familiar oppose the inclusion of any abuse suggestions with the divorce custody provisions of the law. They endorse continuing provisions within the criminal portions of the law and in juvenile dependency hearings—as a protection of due process of law. They had experienced an overwhelming rash of abuse allegations. The chairman of one court's psychiatric panel indicated that 100 percent of the cases referred to them during 1984 had alleged abuse. But after laborious and time-consuming investigation, they found that only 12 percent had any kernel of truth to them. Hence there was apprehension that child abuse was being used as a circumvention of due process and as a way to avoid juvenile dependency or criminal hearings. (Source: James A. Cook, President, The Joint Custody Association, 10606 Wilkins Avenue, Los Angeles, CA 90024. Phone 310-474-4859.)

19. Strong joint custody (shared parenting) laws are a way to encourage cooperation between parents because they set a standard of expected conduct and behavior.

20. By presuming joint custody as early as possible in the court process, parties are impelled to attend to the child's needs, thereby encouraging mature behavior and discouraging divisive, childish conflict, according to Dr. Marlin S. Potash in "Psychological Support for a Rebuttable Presumption of Joint Custody" (*Probate Law Journal*, 4:17, 1982).

21. Joint custody begins with the assumption of healthy parenting and helps promote cooperation and mutual respect, rather than feeding on mutual suspicion fostered by the adversarial system in the courts.

22. The ability to cooperate around parenting issues can be encouraged and enhanced with limited and relatively inexpensive education, counseling, or skillful mediation, according to Joan Berlin Kelly, Ph.D., in "Further Observations on Joint Custody" (*University of California Davis Law Review*, Vol. 16, pages 762-770). Dr. Kelly is co-author (with Judith Wallerstein) of the well-known book *Surviving the Breakup* (Basic Books, 1980).

23. Joint custody empowers women by having fathers share in the child-rearing.

24. Joint custody empowers women because it gives them a greater voice in the distribution of responsibilities after divorce, rather than merely turning matters over to a third party, usually a male judge, to decide.

25. Joint custody is an extension of the drive for equality that is so important to America today.

26. Some control of a sole-custodial parent over children might be reduced, but, through the sharing of child-raising, the overwhelming burden of sole responsibility for raising children is reduced.

27. The feminization of poverty is directly tied to the feminization of custody, as well as linked to lower earnings for women. Greater opportunity for education and jobs through shared parenting can help break the cycle.

28. Some feminists feel that women may have to give up economic "rights" if obliged to go along with joint custody. Yet men may give up even more to get joint custody; for example, they may assume higher child support payments.

29. Parents divorce each other, not their children. Joint physical custody nurtures the child-parent bond; sole custody weakens it.

30. Many sole-custody situations settle down into a quasi-joint-custody situation, with consultation about major issues and liberal access. Joint custody encourages more such cooperation on the part of parents, for the good of the children.

31. In studies of children, findings are that the old pattern of seeing the non-custodial parent every other weekend is not sufficient. As noted in *Surviving the Break-up* by Wallerstein and Kelly (Basic Books, 1980) and other studies, children generally long for the "absent" parent and seek more frequent contact.

32. The natural instinct of a child is to love both a mother and a father. In joint custody, both parents are available to nurture the child.

33. Through mutual sharing of responsibilities and liberal access,

the child is encouraged to develop a good relationship with each parent.

34. Parents have joint custody during the marriage. Why not post-divorce?

35. The best interests of a child is to maintain strong relationships with the extended families of both parents, which joint custody promotes.

36. The current sole-custody system sends the message that only one parent should have responsibility. Joint custody sends the message that both do.

37. The current sole-custody system "gives" the child to one parent (usually the mother) and "takes" the child from the other parent (usually the father). Joint custody allows children to keep both parents.

38. The non-custodial parent is reduced to an occasional "visitor" in the child's life, if even that. Joint custody enables both parents to remain as real parents.

39. Studies show that fathers are as good at parenting as mothers. See, for example, Deborah Luepnitz's *Child Custody: A Study of Families After Divorce* (Lexington, MA: D.C. Heath Publishing Co., 1982). Joint custody enables both mothers and fathers to remain as parents.

40. The studies that compare children in sole custody with the children in joint custody show that the children in join custody do as well as or better than children in joint custody. This, says Joan Berlin Kelly, co-author of *Surviving the Break-up* (1980) and one of the leading custody evaluators in the U.S., is the good news about joint custody. (See Kelly's 1988 article mentioned in Appendix A.)

41. Help is needed to make clear to divorcing or separating parents that they are both legally as well as financially responsible for their children.

42. The "primary caretaker" viewpoint (of sole custody) ignores the reality that, in almost all cases, there are two psychological parents—a mother and a father—and the child knows it. Joint custody recognizes that children have two psychological parents.

43. The drive for joint custody is almost always a grass-roots movement within each state by parents (mothers and fathers), mental health professionals, and grandparents who recognize that children need both parents and extended family relationships for healthy child development.

44. The victims of fatherless families are the children. Delinquency and other problems can often be linked, especially with male children, to the absence of fathers. Children raised by two parents are more likely than children raised by only one parent to do better on a wide variety of social indicators, including higher self-esteem, higher school achievement, and less involvement in crime and drugs. Single parents do all they can for their children, and most children of single parents turn out fine, but, statistically, children with two parents are less at risk than children with only one parent. Both children and society benefit from improved parenting of children.

45. "Ninety-five percent of the nation's 1,000,000 children missing each year are runaways. Many have been rejected by both their mothers and their fathers. We need to encourage greater parental involvement. One way to do this is by joint custody." (June Bucy, former Director, National Network of Runaway and Youth Services, Washington, D.C.)

46. In some isolated cases, mature parties have voluntarily arrived at joint custody, and a judge might approve the plan. But this is a "backward" approach, requiring the divorcing couple to do all the work, without guidelines or presumption for joint custody, at one of the most vulnerable times in their lives—the moment of separation or divorce. Statutes establishing a presumption or preference for joint custody send a strong message to parents that both are responsible for their children.

47. Joint custody law will not affect AFDC eligibility. The U.S. Department of Health and Human Services (HHS) says joint custody does not deprive a person of welfare, according to a study by Donald Johnson, entitled "Joint Custody Arrangements and AFDC Eligibility," appearing in *Clearinghouse Review* (May 1984). To make this unmistakably clear, joint custody statutes could provide that joint custody law will designate a "primary caretaker" for purposes of possible public assistance.

48. Even if parents don't get along, joint custody can work. Given an emphasis in public policy that they are both responsible for their children, they can be thus encouraged to cooperate sufficiently to raise

the children after divorce or separation. Courts in some states have given joint custody in contested cases, against the wishes of a parent. They have told parents that they don't want them to return to court, but, if they must, they should return in a year to tell how joint custody is working and which parent, if either, is not cooperating.

49. Mental Health professionals now overwhelmingly favor joint custody for antagonistic parents. See article appearing in *Marriage and Divorce Today* (Vol. 10, No. 41, May 13, 1985).

50. Judges are gradually being won over to joint custody. Major reason: returns to court are lessened with joint custody, an indication of greater satisfaction. Consequently, there is less litigation burden on judges; custody cases are often the most difficult of all. The conduct of those who do return to court is more amenable to negotiation. The prior sole-custody era had an aura of do-or-die, winner-take-all that requires an all-out litigation and character assassination approach. The joint custody statute implies favoritism for cooperation and conveys an opportunity for all parties to "win" by arriving at an agreement each can live with.

52. Some judges tell fit parents that if one of them wants joint custody, but the other one doesn't, he/she will grant joint custody. The judge states that, if the parents return to court, they will be asked which parent is interfering with joint custody or other aspects of the arrangement. This "nudge from the judge" has helped cases to settle down into a cooperative mode.

53. The National Center on Child Abuse and Neglect (NCAAN), a division of the U.S. Department of Health and Human Services in Washington, D.C., which regularly reports abuse statistics, states that there were more than 1,000,000 documented child abuse cases in 1990. Up to the early 1980s, the American Association in Denver collected statistics from the states. The Association no longer does so. In 1983, the last year for which the Association obtained Congressional funding to maintain statistics by gender, the Association found that 60 percent of the perpetrators were women with sole custody. Another study shows that fewer than 2 percent of child sexual abusers were biological fathers. Most abusers were uncles, stepparents, and other peripheral individuals. Joint custody allows for sharing of parental responsibilities, which can significantly reduce the stress associated with sole custody, in which one parent assumes all the responsibilities and all the corresponding pressures. Joint custody reduces the isolation of children in abusive

situations by allowing both parents to monitor the children's health and welfare and to protect them. Because sexual abusers are rarely biological fathers, the benefits of involving them in joint custody far outweigh the risks.

54. Judges increasingly request couples to produce a plan for raising children post-divorce. Parenting plans are required for divorcing parents in the state of Washington. A parenting plan requires the couples to focus on how they will share responsibility for raising their children post-divorce.

55. Mediation is valuable in helping couples involved in custody disputes. Mediation statutes exist in twelve states as of 1992, up from seven states in 1980. In some of those states, such as Delaware, Maine, Kansas, and California, mediation is required; in other states, mediation is optional. Where it is mandatory, a couple can not appear before a judge until they have attempted several sessions at mediation. Generally, such mediation is successful, and no court battle for custody is necessary.

56. Although many mediations produce some sort of shared parenting plan, not all do. In some cases, the parties voluntarily arrive at sole custody. Whichever the result, the parties have had input into their own plan and are more likely to cooperate in the future regarding their children.

57. Mediation is different from arbitration. In mediation, a mediator helps parties arrive at their own agreement. In arbitration, or in a courtroom, a decision is imposed from above. In good mediation, the needs of all the parties must be addressed and met, so that there is balance and fairness between the parties.

58. More and more judges are using mediation as a way of "cooling down the passions" in order to avoid the violence sometimes associated with sole-custody, adversarial "winner-take-all" battles.

[Note to advocates: Although a joint-custody bill can mention mediation, it is generally advisable, from an advocacy standpoint, to deal with the issues in depth in separate bills. Otherwise, the opponents of either one of the concepts will come together to kill the bill.]

Chapter 3
Parenting Post-Divorce: Problems, Concerns

by
Anna Keller

Divorce and custody wars

The personal chronicles of divorcing parents are known in support groups and the circles of those who deal with the fallout of divorce as "war stories." Each story is completely unique; yet many reveal only in new ways the same themes of fear, alienation, outrage, and helplessness. In addition to the emotional, physical, and financial upheaval that ending a marriage between two people almost always involves, parents who divorce and their children face a whole other set of consequences: how, when, and where will parents and their children continue their relationship to each other? Who will decide these questions? On what basis? What will happen to their relationship as a result?

The fear of losing the chance to love and care for one's own children is difficult to overestimate; unfortunately, that fear is far from an unrealistic one. As for the impact on children of losing the chance to be loved and cared for by both their parents, it is no less, and sometimes more, devastating than the impact on that parent.

People who have not personally gone through divorce and custody "wars" may believe that it would never happen to them or their children: they believe that their own relationships with their children are inviolable; that their importance to their children or their value as loving parents could never be publicly or legally challenged; they believe that they would never be refused information about their child by their children's school or doctors, or drive by their children's house and be forbidden to see them or find that they don't know where and with whom their children are.

To parents who haven't experienced them, such possibilities are nightmares; they sound extreme, maudlin, or just unbelievable. But these occurrences are simply the facts of life for many, when legal lines are drawn between divorced parents. It often takes the sting of personal experience to understand the truth, that thousands of decent, caring parents and their children have experienced these things and the pain, fear, and anger that these experiences beget.

This chapter tries to take these experiences out of the realm of personal tragedy, pain, and loss and analyze not only the incidence (or prevalence) of diminished and impaired parent-child relationships after divorce, but also the impact of this problem—most importantly on the children, but also on each of their parents.

Since it is usually one parent who is cast into the diminished role by court orders restricting their contact with their children, it is often thought that it is that parent's problem: that it is one of the everyday realities (or tragedies) of adult life that must be acquiesced to—accepted—as a sign of maturity. A parent who does not acquiesce is often thought of as a trouble-maker, unrealistic, someone who is abnormally attached to their children, "litigious," a gender-hater, and so on. Yet such a view neglects the interests of the children involved.

The interests of a parent and child in each other are not only fundamental, but mutual. Where one interest must be set against the other, it is the child's interests that are paramount in our legal system and, by implication, in our system of values. What follows will show that the interest of children in maintaining loving relationships with both their parents after divorce is no legal fiction, but a deep personal reality for every child involved. It will also show that the obstacles to realizing this interest are, in the case of most children and most parents, made far too difficult.[1]

This chapter will therefore also address what obstacles exist to realizing the interests of children and their parents in maintaining loving relationships with one another after divorce. Even where both parents are universally agreed to be fit and psychologically and socially normal, where their child is agreed to have a loving and emotionally significant bond with both parents, and where both parents provide the child with decent homes and decent family life, it is not uncommon for such parents to experience untold anguish and spend up to $10,000 or more in legal fees, simply in order to maintain the right to spend a few weeks a year with their children.

What are those obstacles? Why is it so hard, not just financially and emotionally, but also legally, for parents and children to spend time with each other after divorce? Some of the obstacles which parents and children face include:

1. The absence of specific, enforceable orders providing for parent-child access after divorce.

2. The absence of a means of modifying such orders, even where they exist, to fit new circumstances, without resorting to expensive and adversarial court proceedings.

3. The failure of many orders, where they exist, to provide for the (sometimes very high) costs of practicing parent-child access after divorce, including, for example, air fare and other travel costs when one or both parents have moved at a distance from one another; also the costs of maintaining other forms of contact and care (providing sleeping and playing space for the child in both homes, long-distance phone bills, the necessary expenses incurred by both parents while the child is with them).

4. The absence of positive and consistent standards for amounts and schedules of parent-child access after divorce, based on individual considerations but also on knowledge of the amounts and structure of access that children benefit from most.

5. The failure of many orders to concretely address the child's needs, desires, and other circumstances in formulating the parent-child access orders.

6. The failure of many court orders to recognize or deal with the incidence of one parent deliberately preventing or discouraging access between the child and the other parent, even where it has been ordered.

7. The presence of factors which discourage the most beneficial forms of access between parents and children, including the designation of custodial status, the reluctance of the courts to enforce access orders, and the lack of sufficient procedures and mechanisms other than through the court process to enforce or modify acccess arrangements.

There is another obstacle to parent-child relationships after divorce which has often been identified: the problem of parents who do not exercise the rights of parent-child access which they and their children have been given. This problem appears to be widespread, and for that very reason must be understood in the context of the other obstacles enumerated above.

We began by pointing to the pain, fear, and anger that frequently beset the individual divorcing parent as she or he faces the legal restructuring of their relationships with their children. In the light of the obstacles described above, such feelings are far from misplaced. There are, in fact, very few parents who can successfully negotiate one or two, let alone the full array, of financial, emotional, and legal obstacles that are often placed between them and their children at the time of divorce.

Unfortunately, the structuring of parent-child access after divorce is often a negative inducement to actually practicing that access.

First, one parent is usually (in approximately 90 percent of court orders) redefined negatively by the law: they become the "non"-custodial or "absent" parent, the "other" parent, the "contesting" parent. The usual term for access—visitation—underscores the demotion of one parent to the status of a guest in their child's life (and vice versa). (A "visitor's" intrusions in the family are those of an outsider; "visits" by "visitors" are generally at the invitation, or with the express permission, of the family; the term "visitor" carries none of the moral or legal weight that the parent-child relationship deserves.)

Second, the legal system often fails to articulate the specific rights to times when the parent has access to the child or children. Most orders provide for "reasonable" (or "liberal") visitation, with the determination of what is reasonable left to the custodial parent, who may be hostile to the non-custodian. Other orders state that rights of parent-child access are to include specific times, but in practice these rights are defined minimally, as those which have been specified.

Third, the times usually awarded often do not permit the child and his parent to feel they are integrated into each other's normal, daily lives and activities. They tend to award some part of weekend and holiday periods to one parent and the vast majority of daily routine periods to the other. One parent may be cut out from participation in such things as school activities, helping the child with homework, or other activities which normally take place during the week (Scout meetings, athletic practices, doctor's appointments).

Fourth, the process of repeatedly confronting one's loss of this contact and relationship with one's children is extremely painful and can cause feelings of sorrow or loss of self-respect as parents; these feelings overwhelm many non-custodial parents, particularly in the context of other personal strains of a divorce.

Fifth, if the custodial parent denies access to the other parent, even where an order for visitation exists, there are, in practice, virtually no usable enforcement mechanisms or remedies available to the non-custodial parent. This is particularly true where access is described only as "reasonable" in the court order, and wherever that parent's available funds for litigation are limited.

Sixth, as with child-support orders, original access orders are very rarely written in such a way that they provide for any future changes in the divorced family or in the child's age; and the schedule or amount of access ordered for an infant may not be appropriate to the needs of a 10-year-old or 14-year-old child. One, or both parents, may move out of the area. Yet modification through the courts can be prohibitively expensive for many parents, and, if one parent is resistant, the process can be prolonged over several years, producing stress for the child as well as the parents.

It is crucial that we understand not only that parent-child access after divorce should be tolerated, but that it should be actively encouraged. Child access has too long been treated as an issue of much lesser import to children than custodial status or financial care and responsibility after divorce.

On the basis of the research it has analyzed on this subject, the Children's Rights Council, as a child-advocacy organization, takes the position that we need an expansive, positive new family policy that will encourage continuous and meaningful access for children of divorce to both their parents. Much of the research we have reviewed is neither widely published nor discussed in the traditional journal literature of the social research and social work professions. This book is intended to encourage the dissemination and thoughtful examination of both the lesser-known and more widely available research. We hope this will facilitate the effort that we encourage, of family policy makers to eschew bias and cliché, and to begin to deal instead with the realities with which our children and their families must deal every day. By doing so, those policy makers will be better able to fulfill the responsibility they have to foster new policies that will encourage the best possible outcomes for the many children whose parents divorce.

An overview of research on access

The term "visitation" is the prevalent term in both law and family research; it is a term with clearly articulated legal meaning, and it is widely understood. However, the Children's Rights Council would prefer that the term "access" be used in place of "visitation" both in law and in family research, to more accurately reflect the process of family interaction after divorce.[2]

In domestic law, visitation refers to any period of time spent between the child and the non-custodial parent. Access rights are also specified for some joint custodial parents. In effect, while a custodial parent retains substantial legal and determining rights over the child, during visitation the child is in the care of the non-custodian and, absent compelling show of cause, the non-custodian's parenting is unrestricted by the other parent. For all practical purposes, when access is defined, what is being defined is the structure within which parenting by the non-custodial parent will take place: at frequent or infrequent intervals, with or without social or geographic restrictions, in short or long blocks of time, including or excluding certain distinguishable periods of the child's daily or yearly routine—nights, mornings, afternoons, weekends, school days, holidays.

Legal background

"Visitation" rights are essential legal rights of both the child and the parents involved in a divorce. The right of the non-custodial parent and his or her children to have access to each other after divorce is a fundamental, joint right of the parent and child with a basis in constitutional case law, which has held that the rights to raise, have access to, and care for one's own children are "more precious than property rights," are "essential"; and that the right to be with one's children is a "natural" right with a higher moral claim than any economic right. In the past, the right of access has virtually always been raised on behalf of the parent; however the child's right to access is also protected by constitutional law.[3]

Social science background

The legal presumption in favor of parent-child access after divorce is bolstered by substantial evidence from social science research which indicates that post-divorce adjustment of children is linked strongly to the quality of their relationships with both of their parents. Studies show that the quality of a child's relationship with the non-custodial parent is associated with the continuity, regularity, "normalcy," and extensiveness of the contact they enjoy with that parent. Some of the most influential research first demonstrating these findings was done by Wallerstein and Kelly, published in their book *Surviving the Breakup* (1980).[4] This and other research has repeatedly pointed to the "surprising" degree to which children of divorce desired to spend more time with their non-custodial parents; it has also shown that children's on-going positive social and psychological adjustment after divorce is linked almost incrementally to the frequency[5], or alternatively, the duration[6] of the time spent with the parent. Other research findings have pointed to qualities such as "normalcy" or "daily-ness" of the visitation as the aspects which children seek and which make for the most positive outcome of visitation for the child.[7] Whether achieved through frequent, regular, intermittent contact throughout the year, or through relatively long (weeks or months) stretches of uninterrupted daily life together, visitation which is structured so as to allow "normal" parenting activities to take place is most successful. To put it another way: visitation which is structured so as to reduce one parent to the status of a "visitor" (or "sugar daddy," "Disneyland Dad or Mom," etc.) does not achieve as positive an outcome for children as visitation which is structured so as to reproduce the qualities of normal parent-child contact in the intact family.

Other findings

While there is a reasonable level of consensus in the social science literature on the fundamental importance to children of post-divorce access, some policy makers and advocates continue to appear reluctant to accept this conclusion: What is in children's best interest is to normalize parent-child relations after divorce by maximizing regular, frequent, and long-term access between children and their non-custodial parents. But the main arguments against such access center on the question of how such access affects the custodial parent—and only indirectly the child—not how it directly affects the child.

One argument made is that the relationship between the child and his custodian is of primary importance and that no access arrangement between the child and the non-custodian should be allowed which threatens or impinges on the full independence of the child-custodian bond. Not surprisingly, research that has examined the child-custodian relationship has found it to have profound significance to the child. This kind of argument was made in the influential, but now widely discredited, book by Goldstein, Freud, and Solnit, *Beyond the Best Interests of the Child* (1979).[8]

More recent studies show not only interdependence between children and their single-parent mothers but also divergence in their needs. One researcher found that custodial mothers tend to underestimate the extent and warmth of feelings their children have for their non-custodial fathers.[9]

Also, those who draw attention to the economic and social strains often present for custodial (single) mothers frequently conclude that the strains of divorce for children stem (it is implied, primarily) from the loss of economic status and security (rather than, it is implied, from the loss of the companionship and care of one parent). Yet, in a new study (and one that is highly sympathetic toward single mothers), Teresa Jayne Arendell found that the few women who did not experience role overload were those whose ex-husbands had continuing significant and regular parenting roles either as joint custodians or visiting non-custodians.[10] These findings indicate that especially in divorced households whose joint (though separate) incomes are not adequate to relieve one parent of role strain by affording ample paid child care, housekeeping, and other services, shared parenting achieved through extensive access (quite apart from shared responsibility for the financial welfare of the child) goes a long way toward relieving the stresses now felt by sole custodial parents.

Not only can liberal access relieve one parent of the considerable stresses of single parenting, indirectly benefiting the child by relieving the custodian; and not only do studies, described above, show that children benefit directly from maintaining the active, normal pattern of parenting by both their parents; but there is added evidence that suggests that each parent has a unique role and contribution to make to his or her children's lives, since male and female parents tend to interpret aspects of their parenting roles differently (see Michael Lamb's recent work[11]) and since normal sex-role development is related to the quality of the relationship a child has with the parent of each sex. Such findings do not reflect on the personal adequacy of either parent, but rather on the fundamental mental and biological tie that binds children to both their parents for life. This tie is one that transcends many apparent barriers; where these relationships have been hampered in early life, there is a significant need for renewing, rebuilding, and "working out" these fundamental relationships in later life. Children whose ties with their biological parents have been severed or greatly restricted may take years to rediscover and rebuild those ties once they reach the age of adulthood, when those relationships are not restricted by legal orders.[12]

Another question raised about the benefit to children of liberal non-custodial access is the effect on the child of persistent conflict or hostility between the two parents. Evidence of the adverse effect of inter-parental conflict on children (in both intact and divorced families) leads some to conclude that non-custodial access should be liberal only where there is minimal conflict of this kind between the custodian and non-custodian.[13] But research points in the opposite direction, indicating that the many benefits of continued, frequent contact between the child and each parent outweigh the stress that may be caused by such conflict. Such findings lead to the conclusion that visitation should be structured so as to minimize the occasion for inter-parental conflict (e.g., through neutral drop-off points and specific, enforceable access orders); it also points to the importance of removing the issues of child access from the adversarial realm where such conflict (and blaming) may appear to be rewarded, if possible through mediation of parental conflict.

What's really going on

With so many families affected by divorce and by questions of access between children and their parents, it is unfortunate how little is clearly documented and known about the actual patterns and practices of access in divorced families. Little is known about either the content of judicial orders regarding access or about how the real-life practice of visitation compares to these orders.

Research is needed to help answer such questions as:

* How much time non-custodial parents spend with their children;

* What activities and what aspects of the parental role non-custodial parents engage in with their children;

* What the nature and extent is of conflicts and disputes (both formal and informal) between parents arising from visitation;

* How such disputes are resolved, and what the most successful approaches are to resolving them;

* What the costs, both financial and emotional, of visitation are for the non-custodial parent;

* What the extent of denial or frustration of access by the custodial parent is;

* What formal and informal standards are used by judges and other legal and social welfare workers;

* What measures are taken, and which are successful, in enforcing visitation for the non-custodial parents and to what extent these discourage the exercise of visitation rights;

* What feelings and beliefs are held by the children and the parents about visitation in general and in their own cases;

* What legal, social welfare and mental health professionals use as guidelines in establishing or recommending visitation rights in particular cases; and

* What evidence or beliefs underlie these standards or practices.

Research has touched on several, but not all of these subjects.

However, a number of studies, focused on the emotional impact of divorce and custodial disposition on fathers, have described the impact that different post-divorce structures have on fathers, with greater access to their children being key to emotional well-being of the fathers and to better father-child relations.[14]

Other research has indicated that perhaps a surprisingly high percentage of custodial mothers deliberately withhold access to the children from the father for reasons that have nothing to do with the children's wishes, safety, or health. A report in the *Journal of Social Issues* revealed that the number may be as high as 40 percent (according to the mothers' reports) or 53 percent (according to the fathers' reports).[15]

Studies also show that, despite highly publicized claims to the contrary, the vast majority of child-custody awards are still to mothers,[16] and the vast majority of visitation awards are of "reasonable," usually biweekly, visitation (every other weekend). Other surveys have attempted to ascertain the actual practice (frequency, duration, regularity) of visitation in post-divorce families, and these indicate that in the majority of cases (reflecting the limited access usually awarded), actual visitation is, in fact, limited, with many parents not seeing their children even as often as once a month.

The impact of geographic mobility on access has not been studied, although it is known that many divorces (and remarriages) involve subsequent moves of one or both parents, which may mean frequent long-term summer or holiday visitation may not be made, or permitted, as an alternative. Studies do show that frequency of access appears to be negatively correlated with remarriage by either parent and with passage of time (or alternatively, with the age of the child or children, which may reflect growing adolescent independence rather than growing parental indifference).[17]

There is a growing literature on the potential of mediation as an alternative to litigated resolutions of access disputes.[18] Some opposition has been voiced regarding mediation's real effectiveness or hidden dangers for less "powerful" parents, but studies show greater harmony and satisfaction for both parents tend to result even from non-voluntary, court-ordered mediation.[19] There are also concerns about the arbitrary nature of judicial decisions on these matters which might favor mediated resolutions of access arrangements. Judges themselves feel that custody and access decisions are among the most difficult to make, particularly in an adversarial context, presented with conflicting, inexpert or unreliable, and emotional evidence. The dissatisfaction of clients as well as of the judiciary indicates that extra-judicial resolutions will play an increasing role in resolving such disputes.

The judicial dilemma may also promote the search for access "standards." Such a search would encourage policy-makers to review, initiate, or sponsor research to support the development of such standards. One attempt to synthesize results of social research and develop from this synthesis a recommendation of standards for parental access to children after divorce can be found in Cochran (1985), who favors joint physical custody based on children's needs and presumptive sole legal custody in the "primary caretaker," in order to reduce custody litigation.[20]

In another recent article, Ken Magid and Parker Oborn have attempted to develop "standards" for access frequency (but not duration) based on different age groups and geographic distance between the parents.[21] This attempt in turn raises questions about whether standards for access can be developed in terms of absolute quantities of time, or whether implementing such standards (however liberal) would fail to meet the challenge raised by Lowery and Settle, that what is really needed is a standard of flexibility (not of tradition or past practice) in establishing access to meet the very unique needs of different families.[22]

There is another aspect of access which is important but which has received only a little attention: the role that opinions, attitudes, and beliefs play in determining those social expectations, legal standards, and social policies which affect the restructuring of parent-child relations after divorce. A 1985 Virginia Slims poll of 3,000 women and 1,000 men over the age of 18 found that 28 percent of the women and 25 percent of the men believed that divorcing parents should share joint custody of their children. Only 17 percent of the women and 13 percent of the men expressed the opinion that the mother should automatically be awarded custody. If these results are valid, they indicate that society at large is more receptive than might have been expected to the more equal sharing of parenting responsibilities after divorce.[23] A 1985 survey showed that 77 percent supported a legal presumption in favor of joint physical and legal custody; 74 percent supported joint legal and physical custody even for antagonistic parents, provided they were given counseling.[24] Similarly, a 1986 doctoral dissertation showed that "writers with data-based opinions seemed to view joint custody more favorably than writers with non-data-based opinions."[25] Results indicated overall favorable attitudes toward joint custody among mental-health professional groups. Female professionals appeared to view joint custody more positively than male professionals. Social workers stressed the importance of regular contact between the child and both parents more than psychiatrists.

Findings such as these indicate that the most negative opinions about the consequences of sharing parenting after divorce are held least among professionals who work with real families going through the divorce process. The findings also point out that being acquainted with the available research about parenting after divorce tends to more favorably dispose even experienced people to sharing parenting after divorce.

While these surveys of opinion are all about sharing custody, not on structuring access, it seems reasonable to expect that a favorable attitude toward sharing custody would correlate with favorable attitude toward regular sharing of parenting through thoughtfully structured post-divorce access.

Finally, it is important that future research explicitly address the political and personal beliefs underlying social research and social policy literature about access and parenting after divorce. In current domestic policy debates, mothers and children are often treated as an emotional and economic unit, with identical interests, which they may not in fact share, while the mutual interests of fathers and children tend to go without mention. Further, mothers and children are very often portrayed as victims—not only of divorce, but also of their ex-husbands and "absent" fathers. Such a portrayal is simplistic and misleading—it is unfair to many fathers, it distorts the realities of many domestic conflicts, including divorce, it tends to neglect some of the most urgent needs of children of divorce, and it undermines our recognition of women as independent and responsible beings.

Families who have experienced divorce do so as individual human beings, in ways that cannot be assumed from the outset. They deserve to be treated according to their needs as individuals and as members of a unique family, not according to clichés or generalized "knowledge" that assumes they fit expected patterns of dependence, blame, victimization, or irresponsibility.

The advent of "no-fault" divorce, whatever its economic consequences have been, was a step toward demilitarizing divorce and toward redefining divorce as a process of restructuring the divorcing family without creating victims and victimizers, winners and losers. Those who would continue to see divorce as a win-lose battle will bring little comfort or aid to those they seek to help. Particularly, they bring little help to the children of divorce, for whom such designations distort the strength and meaning of their enduring love and life-long connection to each of their parents. Those who put the interests of children above all else are obligated to defend the hearts of children as well as their physical health, and this means putting the opportunity in each of their hands to know the full richness of their parents' love.

Chapter 4
Parenting Agreements— Preventive Medicine

By
Elliott H. Diamond and David L. Levy

How will you raise the children?

During marriage, parents must generally fend for themselves. Almost gone are the days when three generations—parents, grandparents, and children—all lived under the same roof. Then, various family members could serve as buffers and offer inter-generational support for a child. What children might not learn from one adult, they might learn from another; and the adults, like the neighborhood grocer, could be "eyes and ears" for the child.

Today, in marriage, family is generally only two generations, parents and children. There is more responsibility on the shoulders of parents, who in many cases are both working. Research shows what common sense tells us, that fathers are as important as mothers in healthy child development. Children need and deserve two parents—as well as grandparents and other relatives. But how will you raise children in today's complex world, and how will the children and parents function best?

A parenting agreement can be a method of preserving vital family ties between parent and child and between extended family members and children after divorce.

Benefits of parenting agreements

Parenting Agreements can benefit both the marriage partners and society for the reasons discussed below.

A. Some personal reasons for entering into a parenting agreement are:

1. Clarification of values—

through discussion of a Parenting Agreement's provisions. This can help focus the prospective bride and groom and their values and expectations in life. For example, what if one of you thinks there should be sharing of child-raising in marriage and divorce, and the other doesn't. Now is the time to resolve this difference. Such discussions may help you select a marriage partner or might convince you and your intended that you do not share enough values. Better to find out before tying the knot than after tying the knot.

2. Strengthens and stabilizes a marriage—

by making clear that advantage-seeking in case of separation and divorce might not work. The premarital agreement would be controlling.

3. Maintains self-sufficiency—

in the event of a divorce by restoring individual decision-making. With the couple itself deciding on issues, there is less likelihood that the decision will be turned over to a third party, such as a judge or arbitrator.

4. Minimizes expenses—

because making the decisions before marriage can spare much of the expense of attorneys if divorce occurs.

B. Some societal reasons for promoting parenting agreements are:

1. Stabilizes the family—

and reduces the financial burden to the community. Economically, one household is less costly to maintain than two separate households, as the case is with the divorced or never-marrieds. The article "The Deserving Poor," in *The Economist* (April 25, 1987), states that "An American's chance of staying poor is less than 0.5 percent if he or she does the following three things:
   a. Completes high school.
   b. Gets and stays married.
   c. Stays employed, even if initially only at the minimum wage.

2. Reduces risk to children—

by allowing, through agreement, both parents to continue to parent after divorce. "Children of stable families, with two active parents, are at lower risk of using drugs, becoming teenage parents, dropping out of school or, becoming a runaway" (see section on decreased trauma of divorce, below, and remarks by former U.S. Secretary of Education William J. Bennett[1]).

In addition, research reported in the National Impact of Divorce on Children study finds divorce to be a long-term stressor for children. Two active parents can generally do more to reduce the stress than one parent, states study director John Guidubaldi.

3. Lower taxpayer costs—
for courts, judges, and court administrators, when mediation, rather than litigation, is agreed upon as the preferred method of dispute resolution.

Additional advantages for parenting agreements are discussed below.

Decreased trauma of divorce

Few prospective marriage partners are aware of the issues that arise in divorce and the terms of resolution that are best for all parties. They are not aware of an alternative to the adversarial system. Thus, when a marriage fails, issues of property, custody, and support are belatedly litigated in a court of law with spouses as adversaries. The court's decisions often come as a surprise to one or both spouses. These surprises are partially responsible for the trauma of divorce.

These issues, we believe, could be resolved for the most part in a conciliatory manner prior to marriage, at a lesser emotional and financial cost. The mediation process rather than the adversarial process is also less likely to traumatize the broken family. Furthermore, the conciliatory approach makes fewer enemies of ex-spouses. Children also benefit if ex-spouses are less hostile and the broken family remains "related" after divorce.

This means more cooperative custody (joint custody) after separation and after divorce, so that one parent, be it father or mother, is not overburdened with the sole responsibility of child care, while the other parent is a non-participator.

Offers guidance and protection

Upon dissolution of a marriage where children are born, federal, state and local agencies now protect children and families by establishment of administrative remedies. Currently, the federal government (through the U.S. Department of Health and Human Services) assists the states in the collection of child-support payments.

Similar government assistance and guidance is needed to promote and enforce premarital agreements in an era of the six-year marriage. Laws that stabilize marriage through parenting agreements should be encouraged. Terms of the agreement regarding child access (visitation) enforcement, mediation, fair support, access to children's school records, joint custody, and many other divorce-related issues should be included to strengthen troubled families.

Stabilizes marriages and families

Many laws which appear equitable to a single individual may not appear equitable to a prospective marriage partner.

As a case in point, consider recent abortion laws. They give a woman the sole right to elect an abortion. In a marriage this right of the biological mother to choose abortion denies the husband a vote in the birth process. Thus, the legal (and biological) father is disenfranchised.

Agreement on a certain point may serve to give up certain government-protected rights that may disenfranchise the other spouse. For example, you may wish to include in a parenting agreement a provision giving the husband a say as to whether a birth is to be aborted, even if the law gives the woman the sole right to decide on abortion.

Provides a screening process

Making contingency plans for a catastrophe may be the best way to avoid it. However, if potential marriage partners cannot sit down, discuss, devise, and resolve a worst-case scenario, should they marry? Because the premarital agreement is becoming a more popular form of contract, it may be argued that this popularity is a vote in favor of its usefulness and that the parenting agreement is a sensible approach.

The process of formulating a parenting agreement, including provisions that will stabilize marriage, neutralize perceived inequities of law, and elect the forum for dispute resolution will assist each partner in "screening" the other prior to marriage. If there is no agreement, should there be a marriage?

Protects children

How do parenting agreements protect children? Current laws permit provisions for wills that protect the financial security of children of previous marriages, but not the emotional security of children. Knowing that a child will not lose either parent upon divorce enhances the child's emotional security!

Allowing that child-raising provisions will be legally enforceable in the near future, better and continuous parental guidance can be assured to future generations of children who may be threatened by divorce.

A provision that will probably stabilize a marriage is a shared parenting agreement. By providing for shared parenting when a marriage fails, neither parent will have the upper hand in a divorce court; children will less likely be victims in the bargaining process.

Here are some of the questions you may want to discuss prior to completing a Parenting Agreement with your intended spouse:

* Do you want to have one or more children?

* Will you encourage each other to be fully functioning parents of your children, or do you think one of you should have primary responsibility?

* How do you define parenting? Does it include emotional support, providing a role model, taking care of the child's daily needs and economic support? Or is parenting more than that?

* It is expensive to raise children. Who will work to support them? One parent or both? Shall there be a primary breadwinner?

* What form of discipline do you believe in, e.g., guidance and positive setting of limits, punishment, or providing an example? Would you allow corporal punishment by your spouse, school or others?

* What about education? Private school, public school, or parochial school? What of the importance of play for a child? Should play be cultivated and encouraged? Do you both agree to provide your children with activities in the fields of music, art, dance and sports?

* What about religion? Should the child be raised in a particular faith? If so, which one?

✷ What values will you impart to the children regarding honesty, work, family and friends? What information will you impart to the children about drugs and teenage pregnancy?

✷ Will each of you respect the other parent as important to the child?

✷ How much time should a parent spend with a child, in keeping with other responsibilities?

✷ Who will cook for, feed, and clothe the children?

✷ If a child has emotional or learning problems, would you be willing to admit a problem exists? Would you be willing or reluctant to seek professional help for those problems?

✷ What role will grandparents or other relatives play in your children's lives?

✷ Will you read any books about child development, so that you have some idea of what to expect before children are born, and will you continue to read books and magazine articles on child development as the children grow?

Many other topics could be considered, including whether you both believe in breast-feeding, who will take the children to the doctor or piano lessons, where you will live, and who will baby-sit.

Regardless of what you and your intended spouse discuss—and discussion will be very interesting—it is generally best to keep any parenting agreement general. The particulars may change, but the general approach of respect for each other as parents, of shared values, and of a love for children, will not. If you and your spouse believe in a general overall shared approach, you can fill in the details as part of living together.

If you disagree over fundamental ideas, the basis for agreement and working together to raise the children will not be there. One parent may develop a larger role in child development than the other, but if there is an understanding that the child needs both parents, much can be accomplished.

Current law

We need to understand the legality of a parenting agreement within the context of current law. Premarital agreements and related marital laws are obsolete in the sense that they do not prepare prospective marital partners for the reality of a 50-percent divorce rate. State laws do not permit prospective marriage partners to spell out all terms of dissolution of marital issues.

As an example of the limited number of marital issues permitted by law in one state, the Commonwealth of Virginia, see the Premarital Agreement Act, Code of Virginia, in Appendix B. Currently, the following eight provisions are legally permitted:

✻ The rights and obligation of each of the parties in any of the property of either or both of them whenever and wherever acquired or located.

✻ The right to buy, sell, use, transfer, exchange, abandon, lease, consume, expend, assign, create a security interest in, mortgage, encumber, dispose of, or otherwise manage and control property.

✻ The disposition of property upon separation, marital dissolution, death or the occurrence or nonoccurrence of any other event.

✻ Spousal support.

✻ The making of a will, trust, or other arrangement to carry out the provisions of the agreement.

✻ The ownership rights in a disposition of the death benefit from a life insurance policy.

✻ The choice of law governing the construction of the agreement.

✻ Any other matter, including their personal rights and obligations, not in violation of public policy or a statute imposing a criminal penalty.

Past history

Peter Nash Swisher, who recognizes a need for comprehensive premarital (also known as antenuptial) agreements, explains the historical events leading to the acceptance of such agreements:

Until very recently, it was almost a universal "public policy" rule in every American jurisdiction—that antenuptial agreements which attempt to govern the rights and duties of parties on divorce are invalid. This "public policy" rule, stated by numerous authorities, is that: any antenuptial contract which provides for, facilitates, or tends to induce, a separation or divorce of the parties after marriage, is contrary to public policy, and is therefore void. It has often been held that an antenuptial agreement limiting the liability of the husband to the wife (or vice versa) for alimony, or fixing the property rights of the parties, in the event of a separation or divorce, is void.[2]

In 1979, when this law article was written, Swisher concluded that public policy toward premarital agreements was changing and stated that "divorce-planning in antenuptial agreements is a realistic and objective legal concept whose time has come."[3]

The need for premarital agreements is mentioned in several recent publications. It was stated in *The Washington Lawyer* in 1987 that premarital agreements, looked down upon until approximately a decade ago, are making a comeback.

Provisions of an agreement

A premarital agreement must be fair and voluntary in order to be legally binding. *The American Journal of Family Law*, Vol. 1, No. 1 (Spring 1987) said the Supreme Court of Wisconsin in *Button v Button*, 388 N.W. 2d 546 (1986) listed the factors that are required to indicate the fairness and voluntariness.

The agreement must be fair in how it was procured and fair in its provisions. Procurement means that each party must have adequate time, understanding, and independent counsel to review the agreement. Thus, a form of premarital agreement, a parenting agreement, signed by your intended spouse the night before the wedding may be declared void by a court. The courts will generally uphold all terms of an agreement except those that are against public policy and those that are unconscionable. As we have mentioned, issues of custody and access have, in the past, not been included in parenting agreements. However, as more and more states permit joint custody, provisions of a parenting agreement relating to joint custody of minor children may be enforceable at a future date. Likewise, mediation as a preferred method of domestic-dispute resolution is also growing. Provisions regarding encouraging mediation may also be enforceable in the future.

Chapter 5
Help for Families in Crisis

by
Anna Keller

Child-Support Initiatives

Child-support policies enacted over the last five years are the result of the common efforts of liberal and conservative welfare reform movements. The principal aim of these new child-support policies has been redistribution of family income in order to reduce dependency of children and their parents on welfare.

Supporting these new child-support policies have been, on the one hand, policy conservatives seeking to return financial responsibility for families to private parties, reducing dependency on state-provided support by increasing the regularity, predictability, and amount of money distributed to custodial parents by non-custodial parents. On the other hand, supporting the same initiatives have been traditional liberals, seeking child-support reform as a first step in the march toward the guaranteed family-support allowances that have long been a staple of many western democracies.

Motivating both groups has been the dismal spectre of increasing child poverty, particularly in female-headed households, and the apparent ineffectiveness of state governments in enforcing child-support orders.

One of the principal efforts of these policy makers has been to set child support standards or guidelines, state by state, in the attempt to create more predictable and more consistent support orders and also to make these amounts more explicitly reflect the costs of raising children.

Many of these standards have now been in use for at least three years. Their success in achieving the goals of child-support reform is yet to be established. Research questions that need to be answered include the practical effect of the new standards on child poverty, secondary effects of the new standards on economic and legal outcomes, and issues of due process and equity in relationship to the standards and their enforcement.

We do not attempt to answer these types of questions here. Rather, it is our hope to establish that child-support policy cannot be defined in terms of equity and economics alone. Child-support policy by its very nature promotes a range of possible reallocations of family resources, which in turn are based on a range of possible redistributions of parenting time and responsibility.

Most child-support policy presumes, for example, that one parent will provide for all of a child's needs and that this parent should receive financial assistance in this from the other parent. Most child-support policy also presumes that this allocation of responsibility will endure indefinitely and, in general, that the responsibility will fall on the mother, who is presumed to have fewer financial resources.

A child-support policy built around these assumptions will not, for instance, facilitate joint physical custody of children after divorce. It will not facilitate changing custody to adapt to children's changing needs. It will not encourage non-custodial parents to spend more time parenting their children.

As child-support guidelines are reviewed for their effectiveness, it is important to put new measures of effectiveness into the policy equation. Providing financially for a child is the beginning, but not the end, of parenting. When looking at current or proposed child-support policies, we encourage policy makers to ask the following questions:

1. Does this policy result in a reduction of child poverty?

2. Does this policy result in the reduction of family welfare dependence?

3. Does this policy clearly promote the importance of parent-child relationships with both parents?

4. Does this policy discriminate against family members on the basis of marital status, sex, or age?

5. Does this policy make it more or less likely for parents to substantially share child custody?

We urge that any guideline or formula be evaluated with extreme care and sensitivity to the enormous variety of human situations and conditions to which they will be applied. It is critical that these guidelines and formulas be crafted in such a way as to send a message to men and women and their children that responsible parenting includes, but goes far beyond, financial responsibility.

Perhaps the current dilemma that we find ourself in is that we are trying to do two opposing things: terminate a family and continue it. Our divorce and custody laws are designed to end not only marriages but normal parent-child relations. Our child-support laws are geared to perpetuating, however narrowly, parent-child relations. When our divorce and custody laws are remade so that they become a legal means of perpetuating both parents' roles in the family, child-support laws will be less fraught with contradictions, and they will also be less necessary. Ideally, both types of laws should respect the balance of privileges and responsibilities that parenting brings.

Problems with current child-support guidelines

One of the immediate difficulties policy makers run into in trying to establish new, more rational guidelines as to how much support should be paid is the conflicting and poor-quality information regarding the so-called "cost of raising a child" in a divorced setting. What studies exist of these costs reflect costs in intact families. These same studies tend to equate "costs" with expenditures. Expenditures in turn seem to be related primarily to income level and to the number of children in the family. Thus it comes about that "costs of raising a child" are, for lack of better information, equated to the percentage of income that intact families tend to spend on one or more children. This basis for child support guidelines is known as the "income-shares" model.

The "income-shares" model applies a flat percentage "tax" on either the net or gross income of the non-custodial parent. "Cost-sharing" models extrapolate approximate amounts of money spent on children in intact families, then reallocate these costs between the parents, using a ratio based on the respective available incomes of the parents.

The argument against income-sharing based formulas[1]

Proponents of income-sharing argue, on the basis of generalized income differentials between men and women and on the basis of persistent tendencies to award custody in divorce to women, that the father's duty to support should be set at a level that essentially subsidizes the income of the mother or her "standard of living."

This position is inconsistent on various points:

1. It does not "work" (and is attacked by its very proponents) when the income of father and mother is similar, when the mother earns substantially more than the father, or when custody is awarded to the father.

78

2. It is not consistent with the intent of child support awards and fails to distinguish between the purposes of spousal support (alimony) and child support. The determination of spousal support and the fair division of property between the parties to a divorce has a completely separate legal and policy justification from child support, as well as a correspondingly different statutory and case law.

3. The intent of income-sharing is to prevent gross differentials in standard of living in the custodian and non-custodian households. In effect, however, income-sharing formulas do not protect the standard of living in the non-custodian household, since the distribution (or "sharing") of income is developed only in one direction. The non-custodian with a much lower income, different tax status,[2] or other dependent support obligations may be reduced to a much lower standard of living than the custodian.

4. The express intent of many income-sharing formulas is to prevent a drop in the child's standard of living from what they would have enjoyed in the intact household. This is inconsistent with the widely acknowledged fact that the division into two households creates substantial new costs, usually without any accompanying increase in either parent's income. While families with generous pre-divorce standards of living may be less affected by these costs, low- and middle-income families cannot avoid the fact that divorce creates new costs and almost inevitably drops their long-range standard of living from what it would have been in an intact family. Where fault is not an issue, above absolute needs of the child, there is no rationale for maintaining the custodian and child at the previously enjoyed standard, at the expense of reducing the non-custodian to a standard of living significantly below that enjoyed by the custodian and child.

5. Income-sharing formulas are said to bypass the difficult and possibly arbitrary procedure of establishing actual, or ideal, costs of supporting a child. Critics of cost-sharing formulas will point out that those costs vary with the age and number of children, geographic and urban/rural differentials, income levels of the parties, special needs of the children (or parents), rate of inflation, and so on. Nevertheless, income-sharing formulas are based on the very cost figures being criticized, at one remove: they are extrapolated from the ratio of household income to imputed child costs, which in turn are derived from the spending patterns of intact families.

6. While there is a fairly consistent range of percentages of income

spent on children, which varies with household income level and with the number (and age) of the children, these percentages do not reflect the new, higher expenses of the divorced family. E.J. Espenshade[3] reasons that these figures can be used anyway to derive "conservative," i.e., high, percentage figures. But the income available for children in divorced families is diminished from that in the intact family; percentage figures derived from intact households will often overstate the real income level of the family and therefore misstate the reasonable or usual amount (as a percentage) of family income spent on children in divorced families.

7. Income-sharing formulas do not deal with the equity (or practical) issues of high- and low-income households. Specifically, where no "cap" exists on child support, a wealthy non-custodian could be ordered to pay child support far exceeding any reasonable needs of a child (and, incidentally, permitting the custodian's financial contribution to drop to zero). Similarly, where the reasonable needs of the parents are not factored in, a poor or low-income non-custodian could be reduced to dependency by an arbitrary reduction of income, which in turn might be wholly inadequate to support the child in the custodian's home.

A cost-sharing approach

Critics of cost-sharing formulas argue that:

1. Such formulas do not guarantee the two households a similar standard of living. Again, the implicit assumptions here are that the custodian household is female-headed and that the custodian's income is less, possibly much less, than the non-custodian's.[4]

In answering this criticism, we reiterate that the purpose of child support is distinct from the purpose of spousal support and from division of marital property. The purpose of child support is to allocate responsibility between the parents for the reasonable financial needs of the child in each household, when the parents no longer live in the same household. Furthermore, income-sharing does not guarantee equivalent standards of living in both households more effectively or consistently than cost-sharing.

2. Cost-based formulas do not allocate child support beyond absolute or minimal levels.[5] This approach, they say, does not presume the child will benefit from higher levels of discretionary income of the non-custodian, where that exists.

Different levels of expenditure, well beyond a "welfare" or absolute and irreducible level, may be and have been established for different income levels. The income-sharing approach again assumes a non-custodian income which is generous enough to support a separate household, at the same time contributing the same percentage of income to child support as in the intact family. This may be possible in some family circumstances, particularly where the family members all accept some reduction in long-term standard of living, or where other sources of income become available in one or both households; but in the low- and moderate-income situations, the income-sharing formula also fails to guarantee spending on the child above a "basic needs" level. Indeed, there is nothing in the income-sharing approach which even guarantees a basic expenditure level on the child. The cost-sharing approach has the advantage of establishing a clear, mutual understanding of the financial obligations the parents can expect to assume with divorce. In addition, it provides them with the incentive to find other income sources, where possible, which bring their incomes to levels at which they can provide for their children's needs.

3. Actual expenditures on children are extremely cumbersome to ascertain and are prone to over- or understatement and manipulation by the parties or their attorneys.

While there is truth to this argument, it has also been said that no two divorcing families are alike and that "strict adherence to an inflexible formula would cause more unfairness than it would alleviate."[6] Actual expenditures on children have the advantage of taking into account a multitude of individual factors, which, if not considered, could create inequities as real and as gross as the formulas were designed to prevent. Among the factors which must be considered are high and low incomes, urban/rural differentials in regional living costs, shared custody, extraordinary transportation costs, extraordinary medical and other expenses, other dependent obligations, unemployment, and so on. We believe that ideally all these factors should be open to consideration by the courts and that real costs can and should be used to determine what variance, if any, there should be from applicable cost guidelines.

4. Real but generalized expenditures on children (as established in the studies of Espenshade, Turchi, and Olson)[7] are not based on divorced family expenditures or needs and are open to a variety of technical criticisms which raise doubts as to their accuracy or usefulness.

These criticisms are well-founded, and we believe that, for this reason, adjustments should be made in schedules based on any of these estimates. Those adjustments should include the range of individual family factors enumerated above. But it is equally important that estimates of the costs of exercising the parental role as a non-custodian should be extrapolated from the intact-family estimates. This recommendation is made given the absence, as of this time, of reliable data on the costs of children in divorced families or the costs to non-custodians of maintaining an active parenting role, whether through "traditional" or more extensive access. That such figures are crucial to any long-term, objective setting of support guidelines or standards should be clear, and funding research along these lines should be a priority of the federal, and state, governments.

Gross or net?

The only rationale for allocating support on the basis of gross (rather than net) income is that the allowable deductions from gross income would open a mathematical Pandora's box. The alternative has the effect of opening a judicial Pandora's box. That is, it creates inequities as arbitrary and as inappropriate as it is designed to prevent.

Examples of these include:

1. Failure to acknowledge different tax consequences to the parents. Under recently amended federal tax law, there are four tax benefits to being a parent, all of which flow to the custodian and none of which flow to the non-custodian.

   a. The non-custodian must pay all income and other taxes on 100 percent of his child support payments; this money flows to the custodian without any tax liability.

   b. The dependent child deduction is automatically assigned to the custodian, regardless of how much child support is paid by the non-custodian; it can only be claimed by the non-custodian under special agreement by the parties.

   c. The custodial parent can deduct child-care costs from his or her income, regardless of what percentage of these are paid by the non-custodian.

   d. The unmarried custodial parent is also entitled to the favorable "head of household" tax treatment.

2. Failure to account for cost of producing income, as allowed in federal income tax deductions, extraordinary personal medical expen-

ditures, or other irreducible obligations, such as child-support payments to children of other marriages. It is not rational to determine income which is required by the non-custodian to meet ordinary and necessary expenses as income which is also available for support.

Determination of net income (that is, allowable deductions from gross) has a basic foundation in determination of income for federal tax purposes. There are a few other deductions which should be added to make the income base one that is reality-based and logical (e.g., other child-support obligations). In several states, clear-cut specifications of net income are in place, and there is no evidence that these specifications are either inequitable or unworkable. Indeed, in one state (Wisconsin) where gross income is the base, the calculations of gross income, including imputed interest on the value of personal property and possessions, are as arcane as can be found in any formula.

Specification of gross

Gross income (the base from which net income is derived) should be specified in any guidelines or formulas. In most guidelines which specify income to be included in calculations of gross income, the following items are included:

    a. earned money income
    b. income-producing assets

Other states impute income based on all the non-custodian's personal assets, including automobile, personal possessions, real estate, etc., calculated at six percent of the value of these assets.

Specification of net

Once a gross income base is established, certain deductions from that gross income are both equitable and reasonable to determine actual income (and/or relative income) of the parties available for supporting the child.

Acceptable deductions may include:

    a. Federal and State income tax withholding
    b. Social Security tax
    c. Mandatory retirement contributions
    d. Union dues
    e. Health insurance for the non-custodian, the custodian, and/or the child
    f. Child support paid on prior or other support orders

g. Verified and necessary child care expenses to enable the custodian (and/or non-custodian) to be employed
h. A portion of mortgage payments directly benefiting child (for custodian's home)
i. A portion of loan payments for household furnishings benefiting child (in custodian's home)
j. Reasonable cost of repairs and utilities in custodian's home, agreed to by custodian
k. Unreimbursed reasonable commuting expenses for commutes over 25 miles each way

A reasonable computation of net income should account for the relative tax consequences of the divorce, the necessary income-producing expenses of each parent (including child-care costs), and for the reasonable direct expenditures of each parent on other dependents. Such a formula should also allow for the reasonable direct expenditures by the non-custodial parent on the child. This acknowledges that regular access to children is one of the very real, and most important, costs of divorce. In the divorced family, a true accounting of actual expenditures on children must include these costs.

Computing expenses

This is one of the most difficult areas of child support formulas and guidelines. The attribution of income to one or both parents, above what the parent actually received, is a feature of most formulas and guidelines. Most such provisions are intended to deal with situations where one parent (usually the non-custodian) is suspected of deliberately reducing his or her income.

Basing support on cost-sharing rather than income-sharing reflects the need for consistent levels of support and is less susceptible to normal or voluntary fluctuations of actual earnings. A divorced parent who is providing a reasonable amount of support to a child should not be required, any more than a married parent is now required, to seek higher-paid employment (as in the case of a parent making a good-faith career change). And he or she should not be prevented from making other personal choices with respect to seeking employment except those which are harmful to the child's welfare and deprive the child of needed sources of support.

Married people owe no [legal] obligation to their children to maximize their economic wealth. A person may choose to be a judge, rather than a successful lawyer making three times the money. An executive who has earned a large income may rationally change to a different and less remunerative career. A doctor may maximize his income in specialized private practice. A doctor may also choose, for admirable reasons, to do salaried public service and earn far less. A person capable of large earnings in other fields may sacrifice those opportunities to pursue a career in teaching. A person may decide to run economic risks—for example, by turning from a secure well-salaried job to establish his or her own business, in which the near-term opportunities to draw income will surely be less, and long-term success is not assured.

Although such decisions reduce the family income and the children's standard of living, married people may freely make such choices without violating any right of their children. [Under a formulation imputing "potential" incomes of the parties] the same people lose this freedom if their marriage fails. Their children acquire, by the marital rift, an enforceable right to be supported at financial levels which are punitive to the parent whose career choices do not maximize income. If so, to marry and have children would put people's career freedom at risk in an essentially arbitrary way; a child's right to support should not increase because his or her parents' marriage fails.[8]

Another aspect of the same concern is whether income should be attributed to an unemployed (or underemployed) custodian. Some critics of income-sharing formulas have said that such formulas carry no incentive to the custodian to seek employment, even after all the couple's children are of day-care or public-school age. This is (perhaps) a more realistic concern where the non-custodian income is high enough to provide for all the child's needs (even if this reduces the non-custodian to a marginal standard of living). The question of whether the custodian has an equal (financial) duty to support a child, to the best of his or her capacity, is at the root of this question. Equal duty of both parents to support their children is the rule rather than the exception in most jurisdictions, though "equal duty" does not imply equal financial contributions. Some jurisdictions have enacted guidelines to determine the equitable financial responsibilities of each parent.

Elsewhere, if a parent has remarried and remains out of the labor force supported by his or her current spouse, a portion of the current spouse's income may be assigned as "income" to that parent for purposes of calculating the parent's financial obligation to the child. The question of what role a new spouse's income should play in determining child support obligations is dealt with later in this chapter.

Day care costs

The very high costs of day care for children both below and at school age must be addressed by any equitable child support formula or guideline. Any day-care cost not specifically reimbursed by an employer or by a government agency, etc., should be included in any accounting of the costs of raising a child, so long as the custodial parent is employed.

Several of the formulas have broken down child-care costs as a separate item in determining the costs of a child. Child-care costs should be determined separately, since these are highly variable over a relatively short period of time, beginning at a very high level for infant care and decreasing as the child enters elementary school and attends school for longer portions of the day. These costs are highly specific to particular family circumstances and should be treated as a modification of a basic support obligation.

Custodial parent's income

There is no reasonable rationale for not including the custodian's income in any calculation of the non-custodian's child-support obligation. The obligation to support a child is a mutual obligation, and the relative abilities of the two parents to contribute to the child's needs should be as relevant to divorced families as they are in intact families.

Formulas which have been developed which completely ignore the custodian's income (such as the Wisconsin formula) appear to stem from "traditional," but no longer prevalent, assumptions about sex roles, custody, and work. The message conveyed by such policies is that women will be granted custody and that mothers either will not work, or, if they do, their work will have a minor role in family finances. The unspoken flip-side of this message is, naturally, that the non-custodian's contribution to the family is purely, even exclusively, financial.

Formulas based exclusively on the non-custodian's income—all of which are income-sharing formulas—also suffer from the inconsistencies and arbitrariness that all income-sharing formulas do: that is, there is no guarantee of equitable treatment, so long as the assumption is made that income must flow in only one direction: from the non-custodian to the custodian, regardless of the custodian's income and resources.

It is interesting to see proponents of income-sharing when there is a significant disparity between the custodian and non-custodian's income levels. They suddenly become more critical of income-sharing formulas which do not even consider the relative abilities of the parties to contribute to the child-raising costs:

In Wisconsin, Lucy Cooper, an attorney who helped guide the 17 percent formula through the legislature, later attempted to get a reduction below 17 percent for her woman client, a non-custodial parent. Because the custodial father earned $40,000 and the mother earned $6,600, it would be grossly unfair to make the mother pay 17 percent of her income, Cooper told the judge in Fond du Lac, Wisconsin, John Mickiewicz. Cooper was appalled, according to the *Capital Times*, (Madison, WI, August 20, 1985), when the judge ruled the percentage guidelines apply "regardless of income" and that to consider anything else would be too "cumbersome" considering the volume before the court. "It is simply a percentage that I am taking into consideration, and that is that," the *Capital Times* quoted the judge.[9]

Costs of other children

Formulas based on gross income(s) which fail to deduct the established child-support needs of other children are based on a false attribution of truly "available" income and cannot be deemed equitable. Likewise, formulas which fail to take into account new parental obligations, whether for younger children or stepchildren, have the effect of creating two classes of children.

No guideline or formula should be adopted which does not factor in, either through deduction from net income or judicial discretion, either parent's responsibility for other children. Allocations of a parent's resources between children living in different households should not result in significantly disparate total expenditures on those children. To some extent, then, downward adjustment of support orders should be possible (so long as a child's basic needs are provided for) to prevent children of an intact (second) family from living at a significantly lower standard of living than a child from a previous marriage.

Income(s) of current spouse(s)

Any consideration of current spouse income which would have the effect of deterring, discouraging, or "punishing" remarriage of either party should be avoided by any child support formula. Generally, courts have not determined stepparents to be obligated financially for children not their own, unless they are adopted by them, or, in some cases, have come to stand *in loco parentis*. Remarriage is a very frequent occurrence, and the financial, as well as other pressures, on the new stepfamily can be as great or greater than on single-parent families. On the other hand, the benefits of parental remarriage to children of divorce are clear, particularly when remarriage relieves one parent of part of household expenditures; remarriage can also bring emotional support to the parent that indirectly benefits the children of divorce.

Given the great numbers of stepfamilies, child-support guidelines must recognize the likelihood of remarriage and acknowledge its potential impact on the parents' incomes and standards of living, without drawing stepparents into a financial treadmill of parental obligations which have no corresponding parental rights. According to one discussion of current spouse income, "few operational formulas take into account income of current spouses," in part because of the complexity of designing an equitable role for this income and in part "to avoid creating disincentives to remarriage of females."[10] (One would think the same desire would apply to remarriage of males.)

A final aspect of this issue is whether income from a current spouse can be "assigned" or imputed to an unemployed or underemployed (usually custodial) parent.

"Non-traditional" custody or access

It quickly becomes obvious to anyone reviewing proposed or actual child-support guidelines that several very traditional, not to say reactionary, assumptions are being incorporated into regulatory and statutory law, about appropriate respective parenting roles of men and women. The guidelines—in particular income-sharing guidelines—assume that women will be primary, if not exclusive, custodians of children after divorce and that men will be primary, if not exclusive, providers of money to those children.

Virtually every guideline and formula also assumes that the contribution of the non-custodian to the daily or regular care of their children will be so negligible as to disappear altogether from the charts and formulas. When costs of raising a child of divorce are devised, whether based on actual, generalized, or percentage costs, they assume these cost are borne exclusively by the custodial parent.

The negative effects of such guidelines are hard to overestimate. The traditional visitation pattern is the only, or primary, pattern placed before the parties, their attorneys, and the judge. Deviations from these assumptions take imagination, courage, cooperation, skill, and open-mindedness, not to mention money (to pay attorneys) and education (to be aware of alternative possibilities and their benefits to children).

Deviations from the guidelines not sanctioned specifically as being in the best interests of children of divorce will be judged according to the prejudicial standards they embody; if a man's primary parenting obligation is to pay money, and if he is asking for joint custody (which he can only afford if his support order is lower than the "standard"), courts (as well as some outside critics) have been quick to accuse him of "using" his request for shared parenting as a means of shirking his financial ("real") parental obligation.

Fathers are encouraged to believe that their only responsibility to their children is to provide them with money, and they receive no "credit," compensation, or other acknowledgement of either their direct expenditures or their "in-kind" payments.

Several of the formulas that are in use or have been proposed do allow for—though they do not assume—deviation from the "norm." They establish various thresholds for percentage of overnights spent with the non-custodian which justify a reallocation of the child support on the basis of both clear evidence of substantial direct contributions by the non-custodian and corresponding decrease in the expenditures by the custodian. This threshold has been established only at levels considered beyond "traditional" access, e.g., 25-30 percent and more of total overnights.

However, these provisions do not adequately address the need for positive incentives for sharing parenting and financial responsibility after divorce. Nor do these provisions adequately recognize the real costs to non-custodians of maintaining parental relationships with their children, even within the bounds of "traditional" access.

Self-support reserve

To set, as several formulas do, the poverty level as the self-support reserve for all parents raises false expectations as to the extent of income available for child support.

The poverty level is such that a parent is presumed barely able to survive. Only where both households are surviving at this level does it make sense to use this as a base line, and then primarily to prevent the parent from becoming a dependent of the state.

Support orders which leave too little for the non-custodian only invite noncompliance; the state should not put itself in the position of "squeezing blood out of a turnip" in order to try to show itself "tough" on child support—or to increase its federal budget allocation.

Medical/extraordinary expenses

Virtually all formulas and guidelines recognize that children may require medical treatment, special education, or other extraordinary expenditures by their parents. These, subject to review in the courts, should be allocated between the parents on the basis of their respective incomes.

Note that, again, the income-sharing approach is inadequate, alone, to apportion these very real, though not usual, expenses. A cost-sharing approach, either based on actual expenses or based on a general figure with a supplement for extraordinary expenses, deals with this type of situation in a more consistent manner.

Further, in cases where income-sharing results in an unusually large support order (exceeding the usual real costs of raising a child), the additional allocation of extraordinary expenses between the parties, on top of the basic support order, points out one of many potential equity problems associated with support formulas not directly tied to actual child costs.

Geographic/regional cost differential

None of the formulas or guidelines, either in place or proposed, formally incorporate differentials or deviations from support schedules or amounts. The primary reason for this is that such adjustments are viewed both as complicating and theoretical.

Actual costs, at identical standards of living—both for parents and for children—can vary from one region of the country to another (and from rural to urban areas) by factors of 10 percent or more, amounting to thousands of dollars per year. For many families, this is a very significant amount of money and merits serious consideration.

Where a custodial parent's move to another state or another place has, in and of itself, substantially increased or reduced the financial needs of the child, this factor should be reviewed by the court at the request of either party.

Age differential

Studies on the cost of (or expenditures on) children suggest quite clearly that the real cost of children is not uniform throughout their minority, but tends, in the long run, to increase with age. Several formulas, in particular the table developed by the state of Washington,[11] specifically build in different levels of support for children of different ages.

Once again, the income-sharing approach is insensitive to the age-specific, but real, needs of children. While the differential between the costs of an infant, a 4-year-old, and a 12-year-old may not be large, there should be some mechanism, in any formula, which allows for such needs as are real and reasonable.

The larger expenditures on children as they get older may reflect to a large degree the powerful tendency of expenditures on children to increase with available income. Younger children, whose younger parents are at a much lower level in their life-time earnings curve, may "cost" less because the available family income is relatively low. Likewise, older children may "cost" more primarily because their parents, now older and at higher earning levels, have more income available, after basic expenses, to spend on their children. Finally, the larger costs of older children may reflect largely on the increased housing costs of older children, as families attempt to provide private rooms, recreational spaces, etc., for them. To the extent that many post-divorce households are smaller than intact-family households, the reduction in people per household may make these additional expenditures on (larger) housing units less likely.

Number of children in support order

Every guideline and formula developed for child support has incorporated provisions for allocating support depending on the number of children being supported. In general, the amount allocated per child to an order for one child is larger than the amount allocated per child in an order for two or more children. This reflects the diminishing costs of additional children, which tend to drop with the second, third, and fourth child, though there is a countervailing tendency for housing costs to increase the per-child cost as families become very large.

Income-sharing formulas tend to allocate disproportionately large percentages of income to first children, tapering off to less than five percent of income for additional children beyond a certain number, and setting a maximum (in some formulas) of 50 percent of income (or of discretionary income) regardless of the number of children.

A cost-based formula more realistically assesses the expenditures on children in families of different sizes, as they are based on aggregate costs rather than "marginal" costs of adding a child. This approach reflects the fact that the expenditure patterns of families with many children are likely to be quite different from those of families with only one or two children.

Higher education costs

A number of researchers have noted the tendency of non-custodians to cease support payments to their children when they become 18 years old. The same researchers have also pointed out that the costs of attending college, whether public or private, two year, four year, or longer, are escalating to a very high level at the same time that higher education or specialized training has become virtually essential to any young person's successful entry to the working world.

Structuring of child support is, at present, often so rigid and arbitrary that many non-custodians view the payment of support as a legal obligation with no direct link to their child's interests. This is particularly so because the payment is made to the (often hostile) ex-spouse, rather than the child and because there is no accountability for actual expenditures by the custodian on the child. In addition to this, the non-custodian is often discouraged—even prevented, in some cases—from having a meaningful parental role in the child's life.

Therefore, it does not seem surprising that these non-custodians would resist the extension of an obligation—and of a very particular and limited relationship with their child and their ex-spouse—beyond the age of 18. The child's emancipation brings with it the possibility, for the first time in years, of a parent-child relationship unmediated by the law and by legal obligations.

Also, given the expense of divorce, disposable income, which in the intact family might have been put away as savings for college, is much less likely to be available to families of divorce. Disposable income has been dramatically reduced in at least one, and usually both, households. Again, it is not surprising to find that many non-custodians have had to delay personal retirement planning for the same reason, and, when their children reach majority, these parents are faced with a choice of continuing to support their children or becoming, in the long term, dependent themselves as retirees.

A closely involved parent will want to support a child through college or provide other stepping stones to adulthood that meet that child's needs. Encouraging this involvement will succeed better than obligating divorced parents beyond the level that parents are obligated in intact families. There are important and good-faith reasons that parents, whatever their marital status, may have for choosing to support or not support their children once they reach age 18.

This position is consistent with a large body of case law, as well as the formulas and guidelines proposed and in use. Only a few of the formulas or guidelines (e.g., Indiana) incorporate a presumption that the costs of college are to be included in the calculation of support.

Non-monetary contribution of custodian

Calculations of the economic value of the homemaker's services may be appropriate and have been used in determining spousal support. However, custody should not be "rewarded" either by the state or by the other parent, by imputing a "salary" to the custodian for the "services." This is distasteful and personally costly. The financial rewards of being the custodian would also create an additional incentive for one parent to refuse to share parenting responsibilities with the other, for fear of losing their "job" exclusivity.

No child-support schedule should create disincentives to the non-custodian to take an active parenting role after divorce, or incentives to the custodian to inhibit or discourage the non-custodian's parenting role.

Parenting is a taxing, costly undertaking: but it is also a great privilege, and this must not be lost sight of in the debate over how best to allocate the responsibilities and benefits of parenting after divorce. Boone Turchi, author of a major study on the (financial) costs of raising children concludes that the undertaking is so costly in money terms that bearing children is only justified (in the limited terms of economics) by the very large personal benefits derived from parenting:

> A major assumption of this study is that children possess characteristics that, on balance, make child rearing a desirable activity, and, indeed, there is considerable evidence that children are sources of pleasure to their parents. . . Studies seem to have found greater ambiguity surrounding the husband-wife relationship than around the parent-child relationship. . .The characteristics of children that make them of value to parents are not easy to measure or even to list completely. [In one list, however,] it was suggested that children possess characteristics that meet the following psychic needs:
>
> 1. Adult status and social identity (women's major role).
>
> 2. Expansion of the self, tie to a larger entity, "immortality."
>
> 3. Morality: religion, altruism, good of the group; norms regarding sexuality, impulsivity, virtue.
>
> 4. Primary group ties, affection.
>
> 5. Stimulation, novelty, fun.
>
> 6. Creativity, accomplishment, competence.
>
> 7. Power, influence, effectance.
>
> 8. Social comparison, competition.
>
> From this list and from others that might be developed we can state the obvious and note that children play a major social and psychic role in the United States; moreover, it is not clear that any activity that might compete with children for parents' time and money would be as efficient in satisfying these needs

as are children.[12]

This is an eloquent statement of the rewards of parenting, and every one of the benefits of parenting is one which can and should accrue to parents regardless of sex. No parent should be "rewarded" for denying these benefits to the other parent, particularly when the benefit to children of divorce of having active, on-going relationships with their non-custodians has been so widely established.

Theories and formulas which contemplate crediting "services" of the custodian against his or her financial-support obligation are also based on the assumption that the custodian will be the mother. Proponents of such formulas might regard them very differently should a custodial father request "consideration" of his services, or choose to stay home while drawing "child support" from his working ex-spouse.

Non-monetary contribution of non-custodian

The same general considerations and arguments apply to custodial and non-custodial parents regarding the "crediting" of in-kind services against monetary obligations. However, parents of divorce should have the same option that is available to married parents, when, because of debts, unemployment, poor health, or low-paying jobs, they substitute in-kind contributions for purchased goods or services. These parents can often make contributions that will benefit their children. In-kind contributions may include babysitting, caring for children during summers, holidays, or before and after school, providing necessities, making household and auto repairs, etc. These options, automatically available to the custodial parent, who is not obligated to spend, or account for, a given money amount per month, should be available in a limited and discretionary form to the non-custodian as well.

A child-support formula could allow either of the parents to agree to in-kind contributions as a partial or total substitute for cash payments, or it could permit a court to provide for in-kind contributions in suitable circumstances.

Modifications/periodic review

One of the major and very legitimate criticisms of the current structuring of child-support orders is that they are designed to be static, whereas the families and their circumstances are not. The needs and incomes of both households and of the children are neither predictable nor accountable at the time of an original support order. But there are considerable disincentives and legal barriers to both parties to return to court to seek modification of support.

A modification or review procedure should be available which mandates mediation between the parties prior to any litigation. Full disclosure of financial information of the parties should be required in any review or modification process. Accountability for the real or estimated expenses of both households should be expected.

No review or modification procedure should be based on information relating solely to the non-custodian's income. Nor should there be a presumption that modification can only be upward. Again, the presumption here is that the custodian's income (which could easily increase, especially as younger children enter school) is irrelevant. This also assumes that the non-custodian's available and relative income is and will be higher than the custodian's—in other words, the custodian is female and the non-custodian is male. Finally, such a presumption would state, in effect, that children of later marriages do not have an equal claim on their parents' incomes.

Cost-of-living escalator

There are both technical and policy inconsistencies inherent in an automatic cost-of-living-based escalation of child-support obligations:

1. There is no guarantee that parental income increases with the cost of living. Indeed, for the many wage earners, incomes do not keep pace with inflation.

2. Increases in the cost of living, or inflation, do not automatically increase expenditures of households in intact or divorced families. There is no guarantee, in intact families, of a particular standard of living—instead, inflation tends to erode standards of living and to shift expenditure patterns in all households.

Modification or review of support amounts should be subject to review of all relevant factors, rather than depending on a single factor isolated from all others. The impact of inflation on the children's welfare should be subject to an accounting of real costs, in both households. It stands to reason that inflation erodes the ability of the non-custodian to pay as much as it erodes the value of his or her payment.

High and low incomes specially considered

Most formulas and guidelines actually in use recognize that very-low- and very-high-income parents and their children are in positions so substantially different from most families as to merit special consideration.

The reasons for giving special consideration to very-low-income parents are relatively straightforward: to reduce a parent to dependency by demanding a payment which they are unable to make is illogical, even if it means the child becomes eligible for AFDC or other state income supports. Some guidelines simply eliminate the support obligation below a certain level, while others note that a token, even if very minimal, support amount will be ordered, so as to establish the "principle" of support, and to maintain the on-going (psychological) relationship of parent and child through the payment of support.

Cost-sharing models are more sensitive to the real needs of children and the real abilities of their parents to support those needs. Identifying those needs and the parental-income shortfall is a positive step in the direction of establishing income-support amounts and of tracking the transition of families to self-supporting status.

Special consideration to children of very-high-income families is also given in some, though not all, formulas. While children have a legitimate claim on their parents' incomes in both intact and divorced families, that claim is not absolute, beyond certain reasonable points, in intact families; nor should it be in divorced families. Guidelines should incorporate a "cap," based on the reasonable expenses of children at a higher standard of living level. Voluntary increases of support beyond this level could always take place and might be encouraged by incentives of various kinds (e.g., a tax deduction for all non-custodians based on their actual support payments).

Explicit treatment of tax consequences of custody

Recent changes in federal tax law have caused all tax benefits of parenting to flow to the parent with primary physical custody, while none are retained by the non-custodian, regardless of the amount of support paid or the amount of direct monetary contributions expended on the child.

These changes create a financial disincentive for the custodial parent to share, let alone relinquish, physical custody. More important, these changes reduce the ability of the non-custodian to take on the additional costs of sharing physical custody more equally with the custodian.

For these reasons, and until federal and state tax policy is changed, it is imperative that these tax consequences be factored into the relative ability of the parents to support the child. The simplest way to do this is by using the parents' net income rather than their gross.

"Traditional" non-custodian visitation costs allocated

Only a few of the formulas or guidelines developed by the states include any consideration of the costs of active and regular parenting by the non-custodian, within the bounds of "traditional" (one night during the week, and every other weekend) visitation.

Yet, the costs of being a non-custodial or "visiting" parent are much higher than is commonly recognized by men or women who have not themselves been in that position:

> The non-custodial parent also has to provide housing, food, clothes, transportation, and related expenses for the child. Even if the child is with the non-custodial parent for only 20 percent of the time, this means more than 70 nights a year. Where is the child to sleep those 70 nights, on the floor? The non-custodial parent must provide a bedroom [indeed may be required by custom, law, or regulation in some jurisdictions to do so], even if that room remains vacant the other 80 percent of the year.
>
> And what is the child to eat? Clothing, if the relationship between ex-spouses is fairly friendly, can, to some extent, be carried from one household to another for the child, but that cannot be relied on totally. Underclothing and some outer garments must be purchased by the non-custodial parent, as a practical matter.
>
> And what about transportation—the picking up and delivering of the child, medical costs, entertainment, and the like?"[13]

Susan Anderson-Khleif describes these non-custodial costs with sensitivity and accuracy:

> If we are concerned about relations between fathers and children and about understanding the reasons for non-payment of support by fathers, then we need to take a closer look at the financial squeeze faced by fathers during the first months of separation and the first couple of years after the divorce. It is during this period that the fathers face desperate financial problems just as single-parent mothers do, and many fathers withdraw at this stage, setting precedents for non-payment and sporadic visitation that are hard to correct in the future.
>
> Just as single-parent mothers face extra expenses associated with divorce, so do fathers. There are the direct costs of the divorce itself, moving costs, perhaps another car, deposit on an

apartment, telephone installation, and the costs of furnishing the new apartment (even modestly). If divorce comes at a time of economic instability—unemployment, a layoff, a change to a new job—their difficulties are compounded. Many fathers assume the debts built up during the marriage in addition to other support responsibilities, and these debts often make their overall financial situations quite impossible for the first few years after the divorce.

Divorced fathers go through a process of "digging out" financially after divorce. It may take a period of two to four years for middle-income men. Many working-class men never make it—their financial situations get worse as the arrears on their support payments pile up. Some are set back for good.

In addition to the payment of support, fathers find that maintaining relationships with children involves spending money.

Divorced fathers who keep in touch with their children end up with many of the same expenses that live-in fathers have. They pay for many "extras" that have nothing to do with their legal child-support obligations. Divorced fathers routinely find their meager resources are totally gone after weekends, holiday visits, vacations, and summers with the kids. There are many costs that go unrecognized. As we have seen, fathers need a place to bring their children during visitation. They need housing with extra space for the children, and that means higher housing expenses—an extra bedroom, a decent neighborhood, a yard or recreation facilities. Fathers must also stock up on "snacks" and extra food for the kids. They must have toys and paints and books around for rainy days. Divorced fathers who stay in contact with their children soon find that the expenses simply do not stop with the support check. . .A close look at the costs of father-child contact after divorce certainly reveals the "price-tag" of fathering and the link between economic resources and the ability to fulfill the role of father after divorce.

Often fathers cannot pay their support, cannot afford activities with their children, and certainly cannot provide "extras." These financial difficulties have a strong impact on patterns of father-child access. Some fathers can get along—they manage to pay their support and can afford to do things with the children—but many cannot. If the divorced father is "cleaned out" entirely—if he is ordered to pay an amount of support that makes it impossible to meet his own living expenses and to pay for visitation activities—he probably will not see much of his children. He must be able to keep enough resources in his own hands to allow him to lay claim to the social role of father.[14]

It goes without saying that all of these considerations apply to non-custodial mothers as well as non-custodial fathers.

The link between the well-being of children of divorce and the quality of their relationship with both their non-custodial and custodial parent, including regularity, frequency, and duration of time spent with the non-custodian, is so strongly established as to make it a crucial consideration in any formulation of child-support obligations.

Therefore, extremely serious consideration should be given to any formulation or calculation which:

1. recognizes that the costs of parenting to the non-custodian are both substantial and necessary, and

2. provides incentives to one or both parents to encourage to the on-going relationship between the child and the non-custodian.

Income-sharing formulas in particular fail completely to acknowledge that a percentage of non-custodian income must also be used to support the child in the non-custodian's home. Cost-sharing formulas, too, are almost all based on the assumption that no costs accrue to the non-custodian and that all the costs of a child will be incurred in the custodian's home. These assumptions could be made only by men or women who either have no experience of the realities of non-custodial parenting or who believe that parenting by the non-custodian is not important to children—or not important enough to be acknowledged by the state or the courts.

The negative impact on children of policies which discourage and ignore their on-going relationships with their non-custodial parents is a great tragedy, born of misconceptions, stereotypes, and prejudices which would relegate fathers to truly "absent" status within post-divorce families.

For these reasons, guidelines for support should be based on cost-sharing formulas which acknowledge the costs of non-custodial as well as custodial parenting. For example:

1. A minimum of 20 percent of the established costs of the child in the custodian's home should be set as costs which will also be incurred in the home of the non-custodian.

2. These costs should be separately allocated between the parties on the basis of their relative incomes.

3. Access or physical custody beyond the "traditional" threshold of 20 percent should be dealt with by increasing

the proportion of established costs to be separately allocated between the parties.

4. A sliding formula should be developed which relates custodial and non-custodial costs to the proportion of time spent in each parent's home.

5. Until such a formula is developed, child-raising costs in families with access beyond the 20 percent threshold should be determined on a case-by-case basis, with each parent's costs to be allocated between the parties according to their relative incomes.

6. The desire to maintain the child's previous standard of living should not have precedence over the goal of maintaining the child's relationship with the non-custodian through regular and significant periods of access.

An ideal child-support formula

An ideal child-support formula is a cost-sharing formula based on the most widely accepted data on the cost of raising a child at various family income levels, at different ages, and in families of different sizes.

The principles of this formula are enunciated and developed in two significant cases, one in the state of Oregon (*Smith v Smith*)[15], and the other in Maryland (*Rand v Rand*).[16]

Such a formula should adapt these principles to the demand for guidelines as to actual amounts (derived either from tables or from individual calculations) that can be considered "reasonable" to allocate for children's financial needs.

The result is a formula which is utterly simple in its reasoning and principles; which is infinitely adaptable to the unique variables of real income needs and availability of every family member; and which, unlike income-sharing formulas, can be applied to men and women regardless of their relative incomes or custodial status without placing unreasonable and arbitrary financial burdens on them.

This formula does not solve the problem of female-headed household poverty, or for that matter, male-headed or intact-household poverty. This formula is not a substitute for the proper exercise of judicial discretion.

This formula is fair; it does address, in the most direct possible terms, the real economic needs of children; and it does, unlike virtually any other formula, incorporate an expectation that parent-child relationships will not be sloughed off through divorce of the parents.

Some jurisdictions are beginning to use guidelines similar to these.

The child-support guidelines of the state of Michigan, for example, contemplate that the parent-child relationship will continue.[17]

Summary and conclusions

In correcting a perceived inconsistency and inadequacy of child-support awards around the country, legislators have erred. The result has been an almost wholesale adoption of income-sharing guidelines, many of which do not even consider the custodial parent's income, many of which are based on gross income rather than income actually available to the non-custodian, and none of which consider the non-custodian's parenting costs. These guidelines result, in practice, in child-support awards ranging, literally, from the sublime to the ridiculous. To put it in other terms, a non-custodial parent with a net income of $25,000 would pay, depending only on the custodian's income and which state they live in, child support ranging from $304 to $810 per month.

Furthermore, the calculations found in this report do not reflect disparities between how the guidelines account for other variables, such as number of children, low non-custodial income, high non-custodial income, non-traditional physical custody or access, or other family variables.

The immediate impact of guidelines which are widely disparate, which do nothing to encourage non-custodial parenting, and which assess child-support payments out of proportion to either ability to pay or reasonable child need, is not difficult to guess: more child-support defaults, more enforcement procedures, more "absent" fathers, more litigation, more appeals to courts to exercise "discretion." In the hands of an unfriendly ex-spouse, some of the new guidelines are invitations to wreak financial havoc in the other spouse's life. Let no one assume that the havoc to be wrought will be against men alone, or claim that this is the "price that must be paid" for the (implied moral error) of divorce. Legislators, policy-makers, and parents consider their own families, those of their loved ones and constituents, and ask, are these guidelines we would willingly impose on ourselves, on our sons or daughters, on our parents, or on our fellow citizens?

Chapter 6
Banana Splits

Interview with
Elizabeth McGonagle

The Children's Rights Council (CRC) interviewed Elizabeth Mc-Gonagle, Director of *Banana Splits*, a program which helps children of divorced families in the Ballston Spa, New York, school system. The initial interview in 1986 was updated in January 1993.

CRC: Ms McGonagle, please explain how the *Banana Splits* program in your school helps kids, the survivors of the divorce wars. What's it all about? How does it work?

M: *Banana Splits* helps kids from divorced or separated families. Several years ago, we found that some troubled, rebellious high school students were from divorced families. Much of the anger they exhibited was an attempt to "get back" at a parent. Even years after the split, the kids were burdened with painful emotions. The program was started as a deterrent to the problems seen in the high school.

CRC: That fits in with most research on the subject—that the pain can last a long time. How do kids enroll in the program?

M: The program works through peer support. Children bring in other children. It has snowballed from four kids fifteen years ago to more than 20,000 who are active in it now. Since the program is ongoing, the child chooses to come for any half-hour session. We may initially "get" the child the morning after the parents split, through the divorce struggles, right through dating, and to the remarriage of a parent. The child comes as long as he or she wants to. The program is here if/when the child needs it. I think the difference between this and other programs is that it is not designed to be therapeutic. The children meet only one-half hour every other week; that amounts to 8-10 hours during a school year! It's a pure Band-Aid, but it works.

CRC: Pure Band-Aid!

M: In other words, the kids quickly realize they are not the only ones who feel alone and in need of help; they have the shared experience of their peers.

CRC: Do you talk to them in a group?

M: Yes. We meet in groups. The kids range in age, and we may have from 4 to 15 in a given group. They usually meet during their half-hour lunch break. They eat and talk—there may not be a focus on a specific issue at a given meeting. I have a long (10-ft.) yellow paper called a "graffiti paper" hanging on the wall of my office. The kids write their feelings on it. The paper stays up from week to week, and we can focus on that as a takeoff. I'm looking at one now and it says, "I hate mom's boyfriend," "I miss my mom," "I love my stepfather," for example. We gets the kids as they process each change in the family. When time allows there are simple projects on which we work. For example, at Christmas time each child filled an empty 35mm-film canister with various colored pom-poms. This denoted the many different family relationships in which they were involved during the holidays. Another thing that we've done within the school system is this: Outside my office, in a very public place, is a huge tree that has (paper) bananas on it. When a child chooses to join the program, he makes a banana out of paper and hangs it on the tree. Thus, to any parent, teacher, or child, there is an immediate visual impact of the number of kids involved. There are a heck of a lot of bananas on the tree! In addition, the wall is filled with snapshots of group activities, past and present.

CRC: Tell us more about the banana tree.

M: If the child chooses to join and has parental permission, he makes a banana, cuts it out and puts his first name on it. It is a beginning statement of facing the reality of a family change. A child comes to one session without parental permission. We call it a "freebie." It's then up to the child to ask the parent to write for approval for subsequent visits. I'm counting on the child's desire to be in the group. A child often attends the program throughout elementary school. Sometimes life may temporarily stabilize, and attendance will drop; but if, for example, he gets a stepparent, he will often come back in until this relationship begins to stabilize.

CRC: So the program is open to children with a variety of problems?

M: Any child whose family has changed through parental death, divorce or remarriage is eligible. Thus, in any given group, there may be kids at a variety of stages within the "family change" continuum. Each is able to join the group, to "go public" with the fact of divorce/remarriage in his family. Because many of those kids have little control of their lives, the decision to join and come to any given meeting is important to them.

CRC: How much do you charge?

M: Nothing. It's part of the school system.

CRC: How much staff do you have?

M: I handle two schools. We have social workers doing a third elementary school and a junior high. In 1991-92 we had around 300 kids involved. In other school systems that have adopted the program, everybody from administrators to nurses run groups. The staff doesn't need a lot of therapeutic training; they need the ability to let kids "be" and the ability to be non-judgmental.

CRC: How do the parents and administrators help out?

M: Where counselors are not available, the administrators or nurses may have the kids come in during their lunch hour. Parents help their child by their support of the program, which in turn supports their child's need/right to explore the issues.

CRC: Is the main thing just to listen?

M: Yes. Listen and redirect. The kids do an awful lot of monitoring of each other on their own, especially as they get older.

CRC: Redirect what?

M: For example, here is a graffiti paper. On it a bunch of kids wrote, "I hate, I hate. . .my dad, my stepmom, etc. etc." My focus is on: where does hate get you? It's a problem-solving format for the child. Given the situation in which the child is living, what can the child do to become happier? Just learning to cope with specific situations will improve their lives. Talking about it is emotionally helpful.

CRC: Very good, but what can children usually do?

M: Well, the one reaction that's a classic for children to learn is: when their parents are fighting, "not to listen." There's nothing the child can do to change the craziness that parents sometimes display. To listen only produces further anxiety. Or when to tell a parent what is "bothering them." The child learns "timing," when to ask a parent sensitive issues. If there isn't a good time, the child is encouraged to write a note to the parent. These are techniques which allow the child to "take control" in child-appropriate ways.

CRC: What do you mean?

M: Kids learn survival techniques when parents argue. They turn on their radio or stick their head under the pillow, they make up "recipes for survival," or hide in the closet, or sing to their stuffed toys. In the group, kids realize they're not the only kid in the world who has been listening to parents battle.

CRC: Wow!

M: The child also uses visuals. We have a child select a special stuffed animal from home. As long as they need it, this stuffed animal is "their person" whom they can talk to at home when things get crazy. This animal is often named "super-(bunny, dog, etc.)" because it "understands" and can take the anger if the child needs to hit something. It always understands. We're really amazed that this works and also with the strength that kids have to handle stressful situations.

CRC: I'm getting emotional just hearing how you're helping the kids. It's incredible, just wonderful what you're doing.

M: We are thrilled with it and we've gotten good feedback from the kids. Years ago, when I wanted to drop it because of other priorities, the kids kept it going. It was their nagging that convinced me that it must be meaningful to them. And that's where it is. It's a respected group in terms of the school. They're not kids to be pitied at all. At the end of the year, because this is a very public group and one which sees themselves as "survivors," we have a huge picnic. This is to celebrate their learning to cope, and as a reward for the difficult job of sharing feelings. Single parents, teachers and others come out and play kick ball with the kids and eat pizza and banana splits. Very public, very up front. These kids have nothing of which to be ashamed.

CRC: How long have you been doing this?

M: This is about the fifteenth year.

CRC: Fifteenth year! Is this program going on anywhere else in the country? Do you know?

M: Yes. Other groups have picked up the idea. It is throughout the U.S.. . .even Australia is developing a pilot program. A manual which forms the basis for the program can be ordered from the publisher. *Banana Splits* differs from many in that it is not "time-limited" to six or eight sessions, but, similar to the format of Weight Watchers or AA, is always available to the child.

CRC: Where are you located in New York state?

M: Between Albany and Saratoga Springs, the northeastern part of the state. It's a small town where this started, and now we've seen it work in urban areas. PWP groups and a Big Brothers/Big Sisters group have been started in non-school settings.

CRC: To get approval for a *Banana Splits* program do you go to a school administrator or school board and sell them on it?

M: That is all we've done. Other school systems may approach it differently. In a nearby school, a parent-volunteer started the program. The next year she was hired just to run *Splits* groups. Schools recognize that family disruption will affect the child's entire life, including school. Parents are incredibly supportive. Teachers who are feeling zapped by kids not functioning up to potential and by lack of home involvement are also supportive. Administrators are aware that it is a problem affecting many aspects of education.

CRC: Any parents complain about the program?

M: In fifteen years I've had no more than ten complaints. Those parents who are uncomfortable won't let their kids join.

CRC: How many kids have you helped?

M: To date, we've had somewhere in the neighborhood of 80 kids a year; other schools quote similar numbers.

CRC: What's the main complaint of the parents who don't like it?

M: Parents don't like the confidentiality these sessions guarantee the child.

CRC: Parents don't want it confidential?

M: The parents who have problems often don't want their kids discussing matters with their peers. But, most parents are marvelous, that is, the parents who have supported it.

CRC: Confidential methods? You don't disclose what was said?

M: NO. We do not disclose what the child says. The agreement with the parent is this: if I feel there is a real problem, I will get back to the parent. The child knows that I'm getting back. The child always is in control and I think that's the crucial thing. I will first suggest that the child talks to the parent. If they don't, I do. I think that is why so many kids to date were in the program, all of whom joined voluntarily. No teacher or parent can force a child to join.

CRC: The kid can participate after the first time only with the parental permission?

M: Yes. Again, even six- and seven-year-olds can "nag" if it is important to them. They do! Parents almost always give permission. I have even had second-graders try to forge the permission note, when the parent was "too busy" to sign. We've had kids who have left this program start their own groups while in middle school. The kids know what they need/want to talk about.

CRC: Do kids participate before a separation or divorce?

M: Yes. Kids who want to join the program when their parents are financially unable to separate but intend to. Kids in ongoing angry families do not attend. There are too many normal stressful issues that go on in many marriages, e.g., fighting parents. The kids and I know that it doesn't always lead to a split. There's no reason for the child to be involved in this until it's really clear that a split is in the offing. We also have kids in here who have lost a parent through death. Because of the "grief" process, they fit in very, very well. They seem to have an easier time processing a loss from death than many kids do from the loss of their family.

CRC: So the message is clear, you are not alone?

M: Yes. You can survive, and we all will help each other to do it. Because of the group's high visibility and because it is seen as positive, staff and parental awareness of divorce issues has been heightened. It seems that the name *Banana Splits*, though sounding strange to adults, relates to a very positive chord in a child. The huge banana tree has become the logo; the number of bananas visually supports "you are not alone," and, finally, there is nothing depressing about a Banana Split!

CRC: Do you think parents would come back together and not split because of this program?

M: No, that's not the aim.

CRC: I know that. Just wondered if it was a result.

M: We have a parents' group where divorced and separated parents communicate over their child. By opening the group to "all" parents, we hope communication will improve. The parents basically have their own group, and they meet a couple of times a year in the school. They meet at school in the evening and again the focus is on kids, on issues with kids, and how a parent can help kids.

CRC: How often does the parents' group meet?

M: It depends on the needs of the parents; perhaps a couple of times a year. It's run by the parents and the parents request meeting times. Then, a meeting is scheduled.

CRC: Are the workshop groups small?

M: Yes. That's exactly what they are.

CRC: How many different groups meet each time? Does one parents' group meet one week, another parents' group another week?

M: No. We open the group to all parents who want to be there in a given month.

CRC: Well, how can you handle so many in a small group? Do you need a large staff?

M: No. Again, we're not doing therapy. We're doing peer support. Two people, and sometimes a volunteer parent, can easily run the group.

CRC: How many parents in the group?

M: We seldom have more than 20.

CRC: I see. Do you meet with all of them at one time?

M: Yes. They are in different stages of a divorce or remarriage and they help each other. They may break into subgroups and a parent will run that subgroup.

CRC: Is this a full-time job for you?

M: No. I am a school social worker. The *Banana Splits* meets mainly during lunch hours.

CRC: Oh, so most of your time is spent on other things.

M: Yes.

CRC: Like school social work?

M: Yes. A school social worker is basically a counselor in terms of dealing with kids. We cover everything from abuse to "not doing school work." The one thing we've discovered in running the *Banana Splits* program, it is preventive. We see large numbers of kids in the *Banana Splits* program whose problems don't surface in normal classes. Group attendance cuts down on the number of kids who need to be seen individually. Follow-up in high school has shown an ability to continue to use the problem-solving skills and to utilize peer support in a positive way.

CRC: Do you discuss their problems at times other than lunch hour?

M: No. We meet for half an hour per class every other week.

CRC: This program doesn't sound very expensive either.

M: It isn't. We use mainly scraps and throw-ways for the projects.

CRC: Incredible.

M: *Banana Splits* just happened. It has grown like Topsy and I'm thoroughly enjoying it at this stage of the game. I have a manual which

I'll send you and you can get a better idea of the program.

CRC: Thank you very much for your time, for the information and for the *Banana Splits* manual.

For copies of a *Banana Splits* Course Manual, write to Interact, P.O. Box 997, Lakeside, CA 92040. Ask for the cost of the manual.

NOTES

Preface: The Best Parent is Both Parents

1. *The Magic Years*, by Selma Fraiberg (Macmillian Publishing Co.) describes fantasy and reality in young children. The book helps parents to understand their children.

Chapter 1: Children as Victims of Divorce

1. Warren E. Burger, former Chief Justice of the United States. From a speech delivered to the American Bar Association, Washington, D.C., 1984.

2. Susan J. Tolchin and Martin Tolchin, "Dismantling America: The Rush to Deregulate," 1983. On page 20 the authors discuss the adversarial relationship (which underlies our legal system) of the regulatory process. It appears that their view of the modus operandi of lawyers applies to domestic relations as well as other forms of legal practice.

3. Attorneys' annual fees for divorces were estimated by multiplying the following three factors: 1,160,000 divorces per year (1989 data), 2 spouses represented assuming each requires 6 hours of attorneys' time, and an average attorney's billing rate of $105 per hour.

This gives a conservative lower limit estimate of about one and a half billion dollars in legal fees nationwide. The average cost is $1260 per divorcing couple.

The last year for which the American Bar Association gave lawyers' billing rates is 1984 (see *ABA Journal*, Vol. 70, October 1984. Lauren Rubenstein Reskin reported in "Law Poll" that partner billing rates ranged from $90 to $134 per hour, while associate billing rates ranged from $59 to $87 per hour). CRC estimated a conservative billing rate for 1992 at $105 per hour.

"What Fathers Tell Us," an article in *The Squire*, Kansas City, June 14, 1984, reports statistics from a survey of 168 divorced fathers gathered by Divorced Dads, Inc., 9229 Ward Parkway, Kansas City, MO 64114. The average legal fees for all fathers was $5,545, with 53 percent of the fathers paying for their ex-spouses as well. For those fathers who sought sole custody, their average legal costs were $17,323. Using $5,545 per divorce multiplied by 1,189,000 divorces per year gives an upper limit of $6,595,005,000 annual legal fees for divorce and custody nationwide.

4. A. States with Mediation Statutes:

As of 1992, thirteen states have mediation statutes: California, Colorado, Connecticut, Florida, Louisiana, Maine, Michigan, New Hampshire, North Dakota, Oregon, Rhode Island, Texas, and Washington. Additionally, Iowa had a statute that created a pilot program requiring mediation of child custody and access disputes from January 1, 1990, through December 31, 1991.

The majority of the states requiring mediation limit the scope of such mediation to the areas of child support, custody, and visitation.

Only three states strictly require mediation in every case falling within the scope of the statute. These states are California, Iowa (pilot program), and Maine. The majority of states with mediation statutes grant the courts broad discretion in ordering mediation. Michigan, New Hampshire, and Oregon do not make mediation mandatory under any circumstances. In these three states mediation is purely voluntary.

B. Criteria for Mediators:

Only Connecticut and Rhode Island do not delineate any criteria for mediators or mediation program certification. Iowa's statute for its pilot program and the other ten states having mediation statutes, to various degrees, regulate the practice of mediation by requiring minimum qualifications of mediators and\or minimum guidelines for mediation programs.

C. Funding for Mediation:

Only Connecticut, Michigan, Rhode Island, and Washington make no mention of how mediation is to be funded. Most of the states that address the funding of mediation programs place a service charge on civil court proceedings or require the parties to bear the cost of mediation. However, while some of the funding models are similar, each contains its own variation. Some statutes outline very detailed funding models, while others provide only general funding guidelines.

Most of the preceding information is provided by the Erickson Mediation Institute, 525 Olympic Place, 7825 Washington Avenue South, Edina, MN 55435.

A number of courts, such as Baltimore County, Chicago, and various courts in Virginia, use mediation even though there is no state mediation statute.

If you are seeking a private, qualified mediator anywhere in the U.S., you may contact the Academy of Family Mediators, P.O. Box 10501, Eugene, OR 97440, phone (503) 345-1205.

5. Jessica Pearson and Nancy Thoennes, "Mediating and Litigating Custody Disputes: A Longitudinal Evaluation," *Family Law Quarterly*, Vol. 17 (Winter 1984), 497-538. The authors report that:

 ✶ Mediation was perceived as fair and just.

 ✶ A sixty-percent agreement rate was achieved in mediation.

 ✶ Ninety percent of those mediating were pleased with the

process, whether or not they reached agreement, as compared with fifty percent who were satisfied with the court process.

* Mediation reduces polarization for those with some minimal ability to cooperate.

* Relitigation was rare among mediation clients.

6. Ted Gest, "Divorce—How the Game is Played," *U.S. News and World Report*, November 21, 1983, 41.

7. Uniform Marriage and Divorce Act, National Conference of Commissioners on Uniform State Laws, 645 N. Michigan Ave., Chicago, IL 60637, August 1-7, 1970, with the amendments of August 27, 1971, and August 2, 1973. A comment on page 32 by the commissioners implies that, at best, the courts will permit the terms of dissolution to be agreed upon by divorcing spouses only after the marriage fails, not at the time the marriage contract is signed. The comment reads:

> An important aspect of the effort to reduce the adversary trappings of marital dissolution is the attempt to encourage the parties to reach an amicable disposition of the financial and other incidents of their marriage. This section (No. 306) entirely reverses the older view that property settlement agreements are against public policy because they tend to promote divorce. Rather, when a marriage has broken down irretrievably, public policy will be served by allowing the parties to plan their future by agreeing upon a disposition of their property, their maintenance, and the support, custody, and visitation of their children.

8. *Ibid.* The Act states, "The terms of the agreement respecting support, custody, and visitation of children are not binding upon the court even if these terms are not unconscionable. The court should perform its duty to provide for the children." Uniform Marriage and Divorce Act.

9. James A. Cook, President of the Joint Custody Association, 10606 Wilkins Ave. Los Angeles, CA 90024, reported to CRC that as of January 1, 1993, joint custody has been adopted more widely and more quickly than all other family law changes of the 20th century. Cook noted that the concept of joint custody has traveled faster than no-fault divorce, the Uniform Child Custody Jurisdiction Act (UCCJA), or the concept that both parents are financially responsible for the child.

10. John P. McCahey, J.D., LL.M, et al., *Child Custody and Visitation Law and Practice*, Vol. 3 (New York: Matthew Bender & Co., 1983). Section 10.02 states:

> The tender years doctrine embodies a presumption that it is usually in the best interests of young, especially female, children, to be placed in the custody of their mother. Although this doctrine has been largely discredited today as based upon

outmoded sex-role stereotypes, it is still influential in some states, even where statutes provide that parents have an equal claim to custody.

11. *Family Law Quarterly*, Vol. 25, No. 4 (Winter 1992).

12. Ted Gest, *op. cit.*

13. *New York Times*, a report on a ruling of the New York Court of Appeals in *Michael O'Brien v Loretta O'Brien*, December 26, 1985, and December 27, 1985, 1.

14. Federal laws that govern financial child support collection include:
* The Uniform Reciprocal Enforcement of Support Act (URESA), which enforces support orders when more than one state is involved;
* The Child Support Enforcement Amendments of 1983 (Part D of Title IV of the Social Security Act));
* The Family Support Act of 1988, which required the use of child support guidelines in the states, periodic review of support orders, and (by January 1994), immediate wage withholding for all new orders unless both parents and/or the court agrees to a different plan.
* Public Law 102-521, the Hyde/Shelby bill, which makes interstate flight to avoid payment of child support a federal crime punishable by fine or imprisonment. The bill also creates a Commission on Child and Family Welfare to compile information on domestic issues such as access (visitation). The Commission was the result of efforts by Sen. Herbert Kohl (D-WI).
* Public Law 102-537, which requires consumer credit reporting agencies to include in consumer reports information, no more than seven years old, on overdue child support, when provided by child support enforcement agencies. Introduced by the late Congressman Ted Weiss (D-NY) on 9/24/92, passed the House 9/29/92, passed the Senate 10/5/92, without any hearings.
In addition, the Interstate Child Support Commission, which concluded its work in 1991, has made recommendations which Congress is considering to further tighten interstate support collections.
Provisions for health-care coverage for dependent children, perhaps by requiring the parent with the most liberal coverage available to cover the child, is an important consideration.

15. Gest, *op, cit*, 45.

16. Establishing jurisdiction in custody cases is covered by the Uniform Child Custody Jurisdiction Act, promulgated by a Conference in 1968. However, language that established venue when children are removed from a

jurisdiction appears in the Federal Parental Kidnapping Prevention Act (PKPA) of 1980, PL96-611.

17. P. Woolley, *The Custody Handbook* (New York: Summit Books, 1979), 257.

The author states that "up until the nineteenth century, English common law gave the father absolute custodial rights over the children as against the mother. . .[and] the Chancery, acting on behalf of the King's *parens patriae* authority, interfered with the father's custody only in cases of gross parental abuse."

18. McCahey, *op. cit.*

19. Ted Gest, *op. cit.*, 39.

20. Judith S. Wallerstein and Joan Berlin Kelly, *Surviving the Breakup: How Children and Parents Cope with Divorce* (New York: Basic Books, 1980).

On page 125 the authors state:

Perhaps half of the mothers valued the father's continued contact with his children, and protected the contact with care and consideration. One-fifth saw no value in this whatsoever and actively tried to sabotage the meetings by sending the children away just before the father's arrival, by insisting that the child was ill or had pressing homework to do, by making a scene, or by leaving the children with the husband and disappearing. In between was a large group of women who had many mixed feelings about the father's visits. These irritations were expressed in their difficulties in accommodating the different schedules of the other parent to make the visit possible and to protect the child's access to both parents, in forgotten appointments, in insistence on rigid schedules for the visits, in refusal to permit the visit if the father brought along an adult friend, in thousands of mischievous, mostly petty, devices designed to humiliate the visiting parent and to deprecate him in the eyes of his children.

21. "Justice for Both Parents," Editorial, *The Washington Post*, November 30, 1985, A26.

22. All states, the District of Columbia, Guam, Puerto Rico, and the Virgin Islands use the Federal Parent Locator Service (FPLS). The FPLS is a computerized national location network operated by the Office of Child Support Enforcement (OCSE), part of the U.S. Department of Health and Human Services (HHS), 370 L'Enfant Promenade, Washington, D.C. 20447. The FPLS tracks "absent Parents" through various federal and state agencies, including the IRS and state agencies that pay unemployment compensation benefits. The FPLS primarily tracks parents to establish or enforce financial

child-support orders. The Parental Kidnapping Prevention Act (PKPA) of 1980 broadened the use of the FPLS to cover parental kidnapping and child-custody cases. An individual cannot file a request directly to the FPLS. Only state and local child-support agencies may do so. The phone number for the FPLS is 202-401-9267. During the period 1985-1990, the number of requests to the FPLS increased nationwide from 657, 288 to 2,307,274 annually (Child Support Enforcement Fifteenth Annual Report to Congress, 1986-1990, Table 56).

23. McCahey, *op. cit.* In section 13.01 the author states, "Currently, in 90 percent of all disputed custody proceedings the mother is awarded sole custody of the children. Typically, the custodial parent is considered the "victor" in these disputes." (From Bratt, Joint Custody, 67 Ky. L.J. 271, 274, 1978.)

24. Gail Diane Cox, "New Emphasis on Prosecution in Child Support Cases," *The Los Angeles Daily Journal,* Feb. 22, 1983. "Extra radio cars, new court forms, instruction sheets, computer equipment, and even slogan buttons—the Los Angeles district attorney's office isn't kidding about its new emphasis on (criminally) prosecuting rather than suing those who fail to pay child support."
"It's Getting Harder to Cheat Children," editorial, *The New York Times,* January 8, 1987.

25. J.D. Paradise, President, American Child Custody Alliance (9299 Ward Pkwy, Kansas City, MO 64114) in September 1983 reported that child support-order compliance runs about 70 percent to 75 percent, depending on source. Total noncompliance runs from 25 percent to 30 percent. Thus, those who comply with support, partially or fully, outnumber those who do not by about 3 to 1.

26. Statistical Abstract of The United States 1992 Table No. 596, Child Support-Award and Recipiency Status of Women: 1981 to 1989 lists women with children under 21 with "absent fathers" as having a mean support order of $2,995. 4,953,000 mothers were supposed to receive payment in 1989; 3,725,000 actually received payments, of which 2,546,000 received full payment, 1,179,000 received partial payment, and 1,228,000 received no payment at all. This means 51% received full payment, 24% received partial, and 25% received nothing. All figures are based on self-reporting by mothers. However, a higher estimate of support payments made by fathers is obtained from Divorced Dads, Inc. They report that the average obligor pays $409 per month, or $4,908 per year. If this represents a nationwide average, then the total amount that responsible fathers contribute to 2.9 million ex-spouses would be 14.23 billions dollars annually.

27. *Memmer v Memmer,* Law No. 45503, Fairfax County, VA, 1980. As a case in point, consider Memmer's mental injury. Memmer's former wife repeatedly thwarted his efforts to visit his three daughters despite court-or-

dered access. His frustration affected his ability to concentrate on his work and led to high blood pressure, loneliness, isolation, and depression. He was awarded $25,000 by a jury of four women and three men as damages for emotional stress caused by his former spouse.

28. Myron Brenton, *The American Male* (Greenwich, CT: Fawcett Publications, Inc., 1966). This comment also appeared in an article by Jhan and June Robbins, "Why Young Husbands Feel Trapped," *Redbook,* March 1962, 127.

29. Brenton, *op. cit,* 128.

30. Donald G. Alexander, Superior Court Justice, Maine, "Divorce and Child Custody," *Maine Times*, April 13, 1984.

31. Statistical Abstract of The United States 1991, Table No. 128, "Marriages and Divorces: 1960 to 1987," and Table No. 131, "Marriage Rates and Median Age of Bride and Groom, by Previous Marital Status: 1970 to 1987" state the remarriage rate of divorced women in 1987 was 80.7 per 1,000 while the divorce rate was 20.8 per 1,000 women 15 years and over. This means a remarriage rate four times the divorce rate. See also Andrew Carlan, "What Joint Custody Means to Fathers: A Bitter Injustice" *Newsday,* July 31, 1984. The author states, "Wives are twice as likely as their husbands to break up families. In the old days, the man left; today he is thrown out!"

32. Statistical Abstract of the United States 1991, Table No. 750, "Persons Below Poverty Level and Below 125 Percent of Poverty Level, by Race of Households and Family Status: 1979 to 1988." In families with a female householder, no husband present, the number below the poverty level increased from 13.5 million in 1979 to 15.2 million in 1988.

33. President Ronald Reagan, "A Proclamation," *Child Support Report, Special Issue*, August 1983.

34. The "Survey of Missing, Abducted, Runaway, and Thrownaway Children in America," First Report, Executive Summary (U.S. Justice Department, Office of Juvenile Justice, May 1990) reported the following number of children in each category:
—Family abductions, 163,200
—Non-family abductions, 200-300
—Runaways, 133,500
—Thrownaways, 59,200
—Lost, injured, or otherwise missing, 139,100
Although initial reports in each category are higher, the above figures represent what the report called "policy focal"—serious reports requiring intervention by police or social agencies. One reason given for the high number of parental abductions was parents' "disenchantment with the legal system."
The Children's Rights Council estimates that about 6,600,000 children

have their access (visitation) to their non-custodial parent interfered with by the custodial parent, and the government does little to prevent this. The 6,600,000 is based on studies which show that interference with access ranges from 25% to 50% of custody cases. A middle figure of 37% multiplied by a conservative estimate of 18 million children of divorced and unwed parents gives a total of about 6,600,000 children.

One way to maintain contact with your children is by making sure the child's school provides information to the non-custodial parent, as is required by federal law. Federal officials will, if you contact them, let your child's school know of the federal requirements. For information on FERPA, contact the Family Policy Compliance Office, U.S. Department of Education, 400 Maryland Avenue S.W., Washington, D.C. 20202, phone (202) 732-1807.

35. Carlan, *op. cit.* Mr. Carlan hypothesizes that "If the ex-wife gets exclusive custody, fathers will see that these women 'enjoy' its corollary: full responsibility. 'Support them. I'll simply disappear,' fathers will say. The spread of poverty and welfare to former middle-class families now headed by divorced women who heard 'the call of the wild' will reach such proportions that the unconcerned taxpayer will begin to heed the cry of fathers for justice."

36. *Ibid.*

37. Dr. Howard H. Irving, Faculty, School of Social Welfare, University of Toronto, Canada. "Shared Parenting: An Empirical Analysis Utilizing a Large Canadian Base," *Joint Custody and Shared Parenting*, ed.Jay Folberg (BNA, 1984). Dr. Irving studied 200 sets of joint custody parents. He found that 85.1 percent of the support obligors were in compliance.

The Census Bureau reported similar results in 1992, in the first survey it ever made of the relationship between joint custody, visitation, and support. The Census Bureau found that fathers with joint custody paid 90.2 percent of their support, fathers with visitation paid 79.1 percent of their support, and fathers with neither joint custody nor visitation paid only 44.5 percent of their support. The Census Bureau also found that only 7 percent of fathers had joint custody, 55 percent had visitation, and 38 percent had neither joint custody nor visitation. All figures are based on reporting by mothers only. U.S. Bureau of the Census, "Child Support and Alimony: 1989," *Current Population Reports*, Series P-60, No. 173 (Washington, D.C.: GPO, 1991).

38. There are many studies that discuss the psychological and sociological damage of children from one-parent homes. Single parents do all they can for their children, and many children of single-parent homes turn out fine, but, statistically, such children are more at risk to themselves and to society than children who are raised with two active parents. A comprehensive survey of more than 50 studies showing the greater risks (on a variety of indicators) for children raised in single-parent homes appears in CRC Report R123. The risk appears whether the single parent is a father or a mother. A sampling of the research is as follows:

Doris N. Alston and Annette Williams, "Relationship Between Father Absence and Self-concept of Black Adolescent Boys," *Journal of Negro Education*, Vol. 51, No. 2 (Spring 1982), 134-138.

A significant relationship was found between father absence and self-concepts of the boys. They placed less value on themselves, had less stable relationships with peers, less interaction with family members and showed a weaker scholastic performance.

Mary A. Burnside, et al., "Alcohol Use by Adolescents in Disrupted Families," *Alcoholism: Clinical and Experimental Research*, Vol. 10 (May/June 1986), 274-278.

Adolescents and parents in single and stepparent families were found to use alcohol more frequently and in greater quantities than members of intact families. "After adjusting adolescent alcohol use for parental alcohol use, the finding of greater alcohol use by adolescents in nonintact families remained." (276)

Katherine Covell and William Turnbull, "The Long-Term Effects of Father Absence in Childhood on Male University Students' Sex-role Identity and Personal Adjustment," *Journal of Genetic Psychology*, Vol. 141, pt. 2 (December 1982), 271-276.

Males who had experienced father absence prior to age five scored significantly lower on self-esteem, self confidence and social interaction.

Patricia A. Davis, *Suicidal Adolescents* (Springfield: Charles C. Thomas, 1983), 26-33.

A review of several studies indicating that suicide attempts by adolescents are strongly correlated with father absence. One study (Jacobs and Teicher, 1967) concluded that it was not the loss of a love object per se that is so distressing but the loss of love, such as the reciprocal intimacy, spontaneity, and closeness that one experiences in a primary relationship (30, 146). Another study (Frederick, 1976) presented the profile of a suicidal male, in which one of the hallmarks was the lack of a close father-son relationship.

John Guidubaldi, et al., "The Impact of Parental Divorce on Children: Report of the Nationwide NASP Study," *School Psychology Review*, Vol. 12, No. 3 (Fall 1983), 300-323.

Boys from divorced families were found to have lower social and academic adjustment than boys from intact families, independent of socio-economic status. Regular contact with the father resulted in better performance by boys on some measures.

Doris S. Jacobson, "The Impact of Marital Separation/Divorce on Children: I. Parent-child Separation and Child Adjustment," *Journal of Divorce*, Vol. 1, No.

4 (Summer 1978), 341-360.
> Findings suggest that the amount of time lost in the presence of the father is a crucial aspect of adjustment following separation of parents.

Richard Koestner, et al., "The Family Origins of Empathic Concern: A 26-year Longitudinal Study," *Journal of Personality and Social Psychology*, Vol. 58, No. 4 (1990), 709-717.
> The results indicate that there is a relatively strong association between early parenting experiences and adult empathic concern. . .children whose fathers were very involved in their care and whose mothers were tolerant of dependency were most likely to report high levels of empathic concern at age 31.

William Sack, et al., "The Single-Parent Family and Abusive Child Punishment," *American Journal of Orthopsychiatry*, Vol. 55, No. 2 (April 1985), 252-259.
> Abuse was found to be nearly twice as high for single-parent families than for two-parent families and higher in households broken by divorce than by separation or death. Sex of the single parent was not related to reported abuse proportions.

Daniel E. Shybunko, "Effects of Post-divorce Relationships on Child Adjustment," *Children of Divorce: Developmental and Clinical Issues*, ed. Craig A. Everett (Haworth Press, 1989), 299-313. Also published in *Journal of Divorce*, Vol. 12, Nos. 2/3 (1988/1989).
> ". . .[T]he father-child relationship was found to be a good predictor of social competence regardless of marital status. Moreover, the importance of the father-child relationship increased dramatically in the divorced family. This supports the view (Hetherington, Cox & Cox, 1978) that availability of the father is associated with positive adjustment and social relations, especially with boys.

39. John W. Santrock and Richard A. Warshak, "Father Custody and Social Development in Boys and Girls," *Journal of Social Issues*, Vol. 35, No. 4 (1979), 112.

40. Felicia Lee, "One-Parent Kids May Suffer as Adults," *U.S.A. Today*, October 1, 1984.
> Adults who grew up in single-parent homes are more likely to be divorced, have a child out of wedlock, earn less money, use illegal drugs, and receive help for emotional problems than adults from two-parent families, a new study finds.
> The study, by sociologist Daniel P. Mueller and assistant Philip W. Cooper of the Amherst H. Wilder Foundation, is the first to examine the long-term impact of growing up with one parent.

June Bucy, former director of the National Network of Runaway and Youth Services, Washington D.C., states that "ninety-five percent of the nation's 1,000,000 children missing each year are runaways. Many have been rejected by both their mothers and their fathers. We need to encourage greater parental involvement."

41. Dr. Stanley Page, "Fatherless Families Spawning Virulent Form of Child Abuse," *New York Tribune*, June 6, 1984. Dr. Page writes,

A large category of those suffering [from child abuse] are the children of fatherless homes, in which, as the latest census figures reveal, 11 million children are growing up. The homes lacking a father are, obviously, mostly the product of our "out-of-control divorce epidemic." Having opted for divorce as the solution to family and marital problems, our society has created a built-in child-destroying machine. And since there is not, as yet, even the proposal of an idea for remedying the inevitably resultant distortion of the child-father relationship, we can be confident that the seeds of a vast army of sociopaths have been sown. Bred in fatherless homes and filled with boundless and amorphous rage for which they are not to blame, they will overrun this land. They are sure to make it even more uninhabitable for peace-loving citizenry already troubled by major breakdown in morality and by all manner of rampant vice and criminality.

42. Joan Berlin Kelly, Ph.D., "Examining Resistance to Joint Custody," transcript of presentation at the conference "Patterns and Perspectives: The 21st Century Family," Association of Family and Conciliation Courts, May 20, 1982; Judith Brown Greif, D.S.W., "Fathers, Children and Joint Custody," *American Journal of Orthopsychiatry*, Vol. 49, No. 2, April 1979. Dr. Greif's views on page 319, expressed at an earlier date, are similar to Dr. Kelly's views:

Although there appears to be widespread opposition to joint custody, none of the concerns expressed have been validated by research. In fact, there is a growing literature of joint parenting that documents the positive effects such arrangements have on parents and children alike. Children need active involvement of both parents, and the findings clearly indicate that fathers with joint custody are most likely to have a high degree of influence on their children's growth and development.

43. Kelly, *op. cit.*

44. Divorce reform groups throughout the nation report that the two most needed laws for the protection of child-parent rights relate to (1) a rebuttable preference for joint custody, and (2) the enforcement of court-ordered access.

45. Elsa Walsh, "After Divorce Schools Balk at Double Reports," *The Washington Post*, Nov 17, 1984, A1.

Educators, sympathetic to the pain surrounding a broken marriage, nonetheless argue that requests by divorced parents (for two reports) are, at times, far more burdensome and time-consuming than any educational reform ever has been. . .In some cases, parents even run into trouble getting copies of their children's grades, despite federal law.

46. Children's Defense Fund, 25 E Street N.W., Washington, D.C. 20001. Private communication with a spokeswoman, December 4, 1984.

47. Gail Diane Cox, *op. cit.*; Robert E. Kroll, "Dealing With a Lack of Support" *The Register: Close-Up*, Orange County, CA., November 19, 1984. "Orange County's aggressive program aims to make delinquent parents pay, but its critics call it a costly harassment of the poor. . .Orange County's approach: jail for non-payment."

48. Prior to 1985, a non-custodial parent who contributed more than one-half of child-rearing costs received a tax exemption for that child. In 1985, the custodial parent became entitled to the tax exemption, unless a court order or agreement exists between ex-spouses to the contrary. The obligor's love for his child is probably the only incentive for making support payments. Court actions, garnishments, and prison sentences are seen by non-custodial parents as threats and not incentives.

49. If state and federal laws encouraged fatherhood for divorced fathers, over 200 grass-roots fathers' rights, children's rights, and divorce reform organizations throughout the United States would have no need to exist.

50. Justice Marshall, writing for the Court, said that a divorced father could not be treated differently from a father who is married and still living with his child. *Quilloin v Walcott*, 434 U.S. 246, 1978, p. 255. For a more complete study on constitutional rights of fathers see:
Ellen Canacakos, "Joint Custody as a Fundamental Right," *Arizona Law Review*, Vol. 23, No. 2 (Tucson, AZ: University of Arizona Law College), Tucson, 95721.
Holly L. Robinson, Esq. *University of Cincinnati Law Review*, 1985. The author concludes that because states deny the parental rights to retain custody of one's children after divorce a federal law should be adopted to protect this fundamental, constitutional right.

51. Estimates of father-headed households from Census Bureau Current Population Reports Series P20 458, Table G.
Because children may live with persons other than fathers (e.g., grandparents), Mothers Without Custody (MW/OC), a national organization, estimates that MW/OC represents 2 million non-custodial mothers.

52. Geoffrey Grief, Ph.D., "Mothers Without Custody and Child Support," *Journal of Family Relations*, January 1986.

53. Sharon La Franiere, "Child Abuse Reports Often False," *The Washington Post*, November 13, 1984.

54. Private communication from Fredric Hayward, President, Men's Rights, Inc., P.O. Box 163180, Sacramento, CA 95816, 1984.

55. "Attacking Litigation Costs and Delay," Action Commission to Reduce Court Costs and Delay, American Bar Association, 1800 M St., N.W., Washington, DC 20036, 1984. Although referenced ABA study on the duration of law suits covers all forms of civil justice, family law represents about one-half of these cases.

56. Statistical Abstract of the United States 1992, Table 612, "Public Aid-Recipients and Average Monthly Cash Payments Under Supplemental Security Income (SSI) and Public Assistance 1975 to 1989" shows that the number of recipient families increased from 3,568,000 in 1975 to 3,879,000 in 1989.

57. Hetherington, Cox, and Cox, *op. cit.*

Chapter 2: The Case for Joint Custody

1. Joan B. Kelly, "Examining Resistance to Joint Custody," *Joint Custody and Shared Parenting*, ed. Jay Folberg (Washington, D.C.: Bureau of National Affairs, Association of Family and Conciliation Courts, 1984), 39.

2. *Ibid.*

3. *New York Times*, April 10, 1984, C1.

4. Nancy D. Polikoff, "Why Are Mothers Losing: A Brief Analysis of Criteria Used in Child Custody Determinations," *Women's Rights Law Reporter*, Vol. 7, No. 3, Spring 1982, 235.

5. W. Glenn Clingempeel and N. Dickon Reppucci, "Joint Custody After Divorce: Major Issues and Goals for Research," in Folberg, *op. cit.*, 102.

6. *Ibid.*, 95.

7. Wallerstein and Kelly, *op. cit.*, 108.

8. *Ibid.*, 110.

9. *Ibid.*, 121.

10. *Ibid.*, 133.

11. *Ibid.*, 123.

12. Richard A. Gardner, "Joint Custody Is Not for Everyone," in Folberg, *op. cit.*, 65.

13. Catherine N. Carroll, "Ducking the Real Issues of Joint Custody Cases," in Folberg, *op. cit.*, 59.

14. Wallerstein and Kelly, *op. cit.*, 127.

15. *Ibid.*

16. *Ibid.*

17. Philip M. Stahl, "A Review of Joint and Shared Parenting Literature," in Folberg, *op. cit.*, 36.

18. Wallerstein and Kelly, *op. cit.*, 55-95.

19. *Ibid.*, 134.

20. *Ibid.*, 66.

21. *Ibid.*, 68-69.

22. *Ibid.*, 68.

23. *Ibid.*, 86.

24. *Ibid.*, 134.

25. Clingempeel and Reppucci, *op. cit.*, 91-92.

26. *Ibid.*, 104.

27. *Ibid.*, 93, 99.

28. *Ibid.*, 100.

29. Gardner, *op. cit.*, 64.

30. *Ibid.*

31. Clingempeel and Reppucci, *op. cit.*, 95.

32. Susan Steinman, "Joint Custody: What We Know, What We Have Yet To Learn, and the Judicial and Legislative Implications," in Folberg, *op. cit.*, 112.

33. *Ibid.*

34. Gardner, *op. cit.*, 64.

35. Kelly, *op. cit.*, 40.

36. Frederic W. Ilfeld, Jr., Holly Zingale Ilfeld, and John R. Alexander, "Does Joint Custody Work? A First Look at Outcome Data of Relitigation," in Folberg, *op. cit.*, 138-139.

37. Howard H. Irving, Michael Benjamin, and Nicolas Trocme, "Empirical Analysis Utilizing a Large Canadian Data Base," in Folberg, *op. cit.*, 134.

38. Carol B. Stack, *All Our Kin: Strategies for Survival in a Black Community* (New York: Harper & Row, 1974).

39. Gardner, *op. cit.*, 64.

40. Stahl, *op. cit.*, 31.

41. Steinman, *op. cit.*, 113.

42. *Ibid.*, 115.

43. Stahl, *op. cit.*, 31.

44. Steinman, *op. cit.*, 126-127.

∗∗∗ **NOTE**: The following notes, numbers 45 to 64, are reprinted directly from Holly L. Robinson's article, "Joint Custody: Constitutional Imperatives," as it appeared in Vol. 54, No. 1, of the *University of Cincinnati Law Review* (1985). The infratext references, therefore, refer to Ms. Robinson's original text, and not the present text. ∗∗∗

45. See, e.g., Alaska Stat. sec.25.20.060(b) (1983); Ariz. Rev. Stat. Ann. sec. 25-332(d) (West Supp. 1984-1985); Ind. Code Ann. sec. 31-1-11.5-21(a) (Burns Supp. 1984-1985); Ky. Rev. Stat. sec. 403.270(1) (1984); La. Civ. Code Ann. art. 146, sec. A(2) (West Supp. 1984); Md. Fam. Law Code Ann. § 5-203(c)(2) (1084); Miss. Code Ann. § 93-13-1 (1072); Mont. Code Ann. ^ 40-4-223(2) (1983); N.J. Stat. Ann. § 9:2-4 (West 1976); N.Y. Dom. Rel. Law § 240 (McKinney 1977); N.D. Cent. Code § 14-09-06 (Supp. 1983); Tex. Fam. Code Ann. § 14.01(b) (Vernon 1975); Vt. Stat. Ann. tit. 15, § 652(c) (Supp. 1984); Va. Code § 20-107.2 (Supp. 1084); Wash. Rev. Code Ann. § 26-16.125 (1961); Wis. Stat. Ann. § 767.24(2) (West 1981).

46. The legal concept of joint custody has been defined by a number of

state legislatures, in terms that range from the vague and general to the specific and detailed. Some of the vaguest statutes do not contain an express guarantee of equal parental right and responsibilities, but merely provide that the parents share in caring for the child. See, e.g., Okla. Stat. Ann. tit. 12, § 1275.4(B) (West Supp. 1983-1984) [stating that joint custody means "the sharing by parents in all or some of the aspects of physical and legal care, custody, and control of their children." Other statutes provide for equal rights of the parents but are vague about what "equal rights" entail. See, e.g., Wis. Stat. Ann. § 767.24(b) (West 1978) ("Joint custody means that both parties have equal rights and responsibilities to the minor child and neither party's right are superior." Other statutory provisions for joint custody are quite specific about the areas of shared parental responsibility. The Minnesota statute, for example, draws a distinction between "joint legal custody," which includes "the right to participate in major decisions determining the child's upbringing, including education, health care and religious training," and "joint physical custody," which gives a parent responsibility for "the routine daily care and control and the residence of the child." Minn. Stat. Ann. § 518.003(3) (Supp. 1984); see also Cal. Civ. Code § 4600.5(c) (West 1983) (distinguishing between joint physical and legal custody without defining either); Miss. Code Ann. § 93-5-24(5) (1984) (distinguishing between joint physical and legal custody, and providing that in cases in which both are awarded, parents shall "exchange information concerning the health, education and welfare of the minor child," and "shall confer with one another in the exercise of decision-making rights, responsibilities and authority"].

Some states have included in their statutory definitions detailed directions regarding how joint custody arrangements are to be structured by the court. For example, the Kansas statute provides that when a court makes a joint custody award, it may determine "that the residency of the child shall be divided either in an equal manner for the child." Kan. Stat. Ann. § 60-1610(a)(4)(A) (1983). The statute also provides that the court "may require the parents to submit a plan for implementation of a joint custody order upon finding that both parents are suitable parents or the parents, acting individually or in concert, may submit a custody implementation plan to the court prior to issuance of a custody decree." Id. The Florida legislature has chosen to use the "shared parental responsibility" instead of "joint custody," but likewise explains what the term means and how the arrangement may be structured. See Fla. Stat. Ann. § 61.13(2)(a) (Supp. 1970-1985) (providing that "in ordering shared parental responsibility, the court may consider the expressed desires of the parents and may grant to one party the ultimate responsibility over specific aspects of the child's welfare or may divide those aspects between the parties based on the best interests of the child").

47. See infra text accompanying notes 52-65.

48. See, e.g., Fla. Stat. Ann. § 63.13(2) (Supp. 1970-1983); Idaho Code § 32-717B(4) (West Supp. 1984); La. Civ. Code Ann. art. 146(C) (West Supp. 1984).

49. See infra notes 25-32 and accompanying text.

50. See, e.g., Folberg & Graham, Joint Custody of Children Following Divorce, 12 U.C.D. L. Rev. 523 (1979); Miller, Joint Custody, 13 Fam. L.Q. 345(1979); Ramey, Stender & smaller, Joint Custody: Are Two Homes Better Than One?, 8 Women's L.F. 559 (1979); Robinson, Joint Custody: An Idea Whose Time Has Come, 21 J. Fam. L. 641 (1983); Trombetta, Joint Custody: Recent Research and Overloaded Courtrooms Inspire New Solutions to Custody Disputes, 19 J. Fam. L. 213 (1980); Note, Joint Custody: A Revolution in Child Custody Law?, 20 Washburn L.J. 326 (1981); Comment, Joint Custody: An Alternative for Divorced Parents, 26 UCLA L. Rev. 1084 (1979).

51. For example, the California statute authorizing joint custody speaks in the broad terms of legislative policy by providing that joint custody entitles the parents to share in physical custody of the child "in such a way as to assure the child or children of frequent and continuing contact with both parents." Cal. Civ. Code § 4600.5(c) (West 1983).

52. See, e.g., Ill. Ann. Stat. ch. 3, §132 (Smith-Hurd 1978); Ky. Rev. Stat. § 405.020(1) (1984); Md. Fam. Law Code Ann. § 5-201(B)(2 (1984).

53. Several states by statute have provided that a court may grant exclusive decision-making authority to the custodial parent. See, e.g., Kan. Stat. Ann. § 60-1610(a(4)(B) (1983) ("The custodial parent shall have the right to make decisions in the best interests of the child, subject to the visitation rights of the non-custodial parent."); Minn. Stat. Ann. § 528.003(3) (West Supp. 1984) ("'Legal custody' means the right to determine the child's upbringing, including education, health care and religious training."); Miss. Code Ann. § 93-5-24(5)(d) (West Supp. 1984) ("'Legal custody' means the decision-making rights, the responsibilities and the authority relating to the health, education and welfare of a child.")

In a few states with no express statutory provision on the subject, the same rule is reflected in judicial decisions, which typically grant the custodial parent exclusive control over the discipline, education and religious training of the child. The approach of the New Jersey courts is fairly typical of the approaches taken in other states. See, e.g., Esposito v Esposito, 41 N.J. 143, 146, 195 A.2d 295, 297 (1963) (enunciating rule, with regard to child's religious training, that "[c]ustody normally carries with it full control of the child's religious upbringing. At this time there is no occasion for considering when, if ever, a court would be justified in interfering with the custodian's religious selection and guidance"); see also Pogue v Pogue, 147, N.J. Super. 61, 63, 370 A.2d 539, 540-41 (Ch. Div. 1977) (This court will not interfere. . .with the day-to-day discipline of the custodial parent unless some basic problem involving the welfare of the child is involved."); Schumm v Schumm, 122 N.J. Super. 146, 150, 299, A.2d 423, 426 (1973) ([The] custodian has the right to determine the kind of education which is suitable to the child entrusted to its care."); Boerger v Boerger, 26 N.J. Super. 90, 104, 97 A.2d 419, 427 (Ch. Div. 1953) (stating, in course of finding custodial parent free to control child's life without interference from non-custodial parent, that "[t]he parent to whom child is awarded must logically and naturally be the one who lawfully exercises the greater control and influence over the child. The mother, who lives with the child more than six days a week, as contrasted with the father's limited visitation of a few hours on Sunday, is the one who actually rears the child and shapes its moral, mental, emotional, and physical nature.")

54. Various commentators have discussed the fact that evidence indicates that the traditional sole-custody system has an adverse impact both on the child and on the parents. For example, it is recognized that sole custody imposes significant burdens on the custodial parent, who most often is the child's mother. See Folberg & Graham, supra note 50, at 553-54. A mother with sole custody might tend to feel over-burdened and exhausted, with the result that the mother becomes socially isolated. Id. It is often difficult for a divorced mother to establish a career and to break free of her financial dependence upon the former spouse. A child living in such an arrangement may sense the strains felt by the mother and, accordingly, may feel that he is a burden. Miller, supra note 50, at 356-57; Trombetta, supra note 50, at 221-22; Comment, supra note 50, at 1115.

In addition, sole custody arrangements often have a harmful effect on the non-custodial parent. As one commentator has stated: "If mothers feel 'over-burdened' following divorce, fathers usually are not sufficiently 'burdened.'" Folberg & Graham, supra note 50, at 555. In addition to the stress and sense of loss that frequently overwhelm men following any divorce, the adjustment from home and family to the limitations of access rights and support obligations, with none of the attendant rewards of continuing contact with one's children, may make a divorced father give up the attempt to maintain contact with his children. See id. Even if the father continues to see his children through periodic visits, the father-child bond characteristically is a weak one, because of the fact that the father is seen by the children only as an infrequent visitor and not as a feature of everyday life. See Miller, supra note 50, at 455-56.

Evidence also supports the conclusion that the traditional sole custody arrangement has a detrimental effect on children. One commentator has identified the following problems with that arrangement: feelings of loss and abandonment, strained interactions with both parents, disturbance in cognitive performance, and sex-role identification problems. See Trombetta, supra note 50, at 217-20; see also Miller, supra note 50, at 354-59; Robinson, supra note 50, at 644-49; Trombetta, supra note 50, at 215-17, 220-24; Comment, supra note 50. at 1113-17.

55. See. Miller, supra note 50, at 403, 411; Robinson, supra note 50, at 645-46; Trombetta, supra note 50, at 230-31: Note, supra note 50, at 332-33.

56. One commentator asserts that "joint custody provides the most continuous, loving situation for the child. . .That child sees that both parents

continue to love him enough to want to retain custody of him, and he sees that he can love one parent without being disloyal to the other." Note, supra note 50, at 333-34. Others have noted that "[s]ome experts believe that joint custody, by reducing the child's feelings of rejection and abandonment, as well as supplying continued positive role models, is conducive to the child's emotional stability." Folberg & Graham, supra note 50, at 557; see also Miller, supra note 50, at 362-64; Robinson, supra note 50, at 650; supra note 54 (listing commentators' discussions of harms to child resulting from sole custody arrangements).

57. See supra note 54 (discussing adverse effects of sole custody on custodial parent and on non-custodial parent).

58. A joint custody arrangement may allow a mother, who otherwise might have been burdened with the responsibilities of sole custody, the opportunity to establish her financial independence and to develop a life outside of her home. At the same time, the arrangement will help to assuage the guilt that the mother might feel if she ceded sole custody to the child's father in order to avoid the pressures of full-time custody. See Folberg & Graham, supra note 50, at 553-54. The parent who might otherwise not have been awarded custody will likewise benefit from the chance to participate in his child's upbringing. This benefit might in turn help the child, in that a parent who enjoys sharing in the moral and legal obligations of parenthood may be more apt to take seriously the financial obligations of parenthood. See Note, supra note 50, at 333; Miller, supra note 6, at 365.

59. Joint custody may alleviate some of the struggles between divorced parents because of the fact that the child no longer is in an environment where it is necessary for him to "choose" between his parents, and, accordingly, the parents will feel less fear of rejection. Comment, supra note 50, at 1116; see also Folberg & Graham, supra note 50, at 554-55.

60. Comment, supra note 50, at 1108.

61. See M. Roman & W. Haddad, *The Disposable Parent: The Case for Joint Custody* 52 (1978); Ramey, Stender & Smaller, supra note 50, at 574.

62. See supra note 54.

63. Granting a hostile and bitter parent exclusive decision-making authority and physical possession of the child arguably places that parent in a superior legal position to the other parent and thus may give the custodial parent great power over the non-custodial parent. The custodial parent can use his rights to make the child unavailable to spend time with the non-custodial parent, for example, if he organizes such a full schedule of educational and social activities for the child that there is no time left for weekly visits with the other parent. The parent in custody may fend off attempts by the other parent

to see the child by claiming that visits by the non-custodial parent disrupt the child's routine or interfere with the child's discipline. Such tactics can result in an ever-widening gulf between the non-custodial parent and the child and are, to a large extent, the sort of acts with which a court is powerless to interfere. See Miller, supra note 50, at 355-56 (noting that a custodial mother often can employ "blackmail and vengeful tactics" against a father trying to maintain contact with his child); see also Robinson, supra note 50, at 670-72. Arguably, a joint-custody award, by establishing comparable legal rights in both parents, would go a long way toward preventing this potential for abuse and would allow each parent a more meaningful opportunity to protect his rights in court. See Trombetta, supra note 50, at 233 (stating that "[e]ven when parties are highly antagonistic, the court can still protect each parent's right to be a parent, and each parent's obligation not to interfere in the areas delegated to the other party"); see also Robinson, supra note 50, at 679-80.

64. A variety of options, including counseling and mediation, are available to aid divorced couples having difficulty in reconciling their hostilities toward the former spouse with their continuing obligations as parent. To the extent that continuing conflict between parents endangers a court-imposed custody arrangement, the court should require that parents take advantage of such options. See Robinson, supra note 50, at 655; Trombetta, supra note 6, at 232-33. It is possible that parents who have made a commitment to a joint custody arrangement to some extent already have demonstrated their good faith and willingness to work together for the benefit of their child. See Folberg & Graham, supra note 50, at 550.

***NOTE: The above footnotes 45-64 are from Holly Robinson's 1985 article. For an update of state joint custody (shared parenting) laws as of 1992, see Appendix B.

Chapter 3: Parenting Post-Divorce: Problems, Concerns

1. The pattern of awarding custody to one parent and of making the other parent legally a non-parent, with greatly reduced parental responsibilities and privileges, is one to which CRC is deeply opposed. CRC's review of research on the relative benefits to children of joint and sole custody (see CRC Report R-103A, 1987, Synopses of Sole and Joint Custody Studies) shows that the preponderance of research supports the presumption that joint custody is in the best interests of children of divorce, primarily for the reason that joint custody both facilitates and encourages liberal access for children to both of their parents. Thus the arguments for joint custody and for expansive post-divorce access often converge, both in the present report and in research findings.

2. At CRC's suggestions, the U.S. Congress used the word "access" in Section 504 of the 1988 Family Support Act (P.L. 100-485), in which Congress authorized $8 million for access (visitation) demonstration projects in various states. CRC had testified before several Congressional Committees that non-

custodial parents are not "visitors" in their children's lives, and that "access" focuses on the child's rights, as well.

. An excellent review of the constitutional basis for the right of parent-child access after divorce can be found in Steven L. Novinson, "Post-divorce Visitation: Untying the Triangular Knot," *University of Illinois Law Review*, 1983, 121-200.

4. Wallerstein and Kelly, *op. cit.*

5. See Wallerstein and Kelly, "The Effects of Parental Divorce: Experiences of the Child in Early Latency," *American Journal of Orthopsychiatry*, Vol. 20 (1976); also see Victoria Beech Lublin, *The Relationship Between the Physical Accessibility and Responsiveness of Attachment Figures with Child Adjustment Following Divorce* (Doctoral Dissertation, New York University, 1983). UMI Order No. 83-25224., and reviews of social science findings on this topic in Steven L. Novinson, *op. cit.*, and Robert F. Cochran, "The Search for Guidance in Determining the Best Interests of the Child at Divorce: Reconciling the Primary Caretaker and Joint Custody Preferences," *University of Richmond Law Review*, Vol. 20, No. 1 (Fall 1985), 1-65. By 1989, Wallerstein and Kelly had published separate follow-up studies of their earlier findings. Kelly's have been abstracted in the next section of this report; Wallerstein's is considered methodologically questionable, particularly reflecting an abnormal sample which cannot safely be generalized to the population of divorced families and their children.

6. See John M. Palen, *An Analysis of the Father-Son Relationship in Post-divorce Mother-custody Families* (Doctoral Dissertation, University of Chicago, 1985). See also Robert D. Hess and Kathleen A. Camara, "Post-divorce Family Relationships as Mediating Factors in the Consequences of Divorce for Children," *Journal of Social Issues*, Vol. 5 No. 4 (1979), 79-96.

7. See Allyson Walker, *Satisfaction of Adolescents Experiencing Various Patterns of Visitation with Their Divorced Fathers* (Doctoral Dissertation, Harvard University, 1985). UMI Order No. 86-1988. See also Cochran, *op. cit.*, 44-58.

8. See, for instance, Steven Novinson's thorough review of the "BBI" (Beyond the Best Interests of the Child) Thesis, and of the empirical and other critical responses to the claims of the BBI authors, in his article, "Post-Divorce Visitation: Untying the Triangular Knot," *University of Illinois Law Review*, 1983, No. 1, especially at 141-155.

9. Tracy Barr Grossman, *Mothers and Children Facing Divorce*, (UMI Research Press, 1986; Revision of doctoral dissertation, University of Michigan, 1984), 153.

10. See Teresa Jayne Arendell, "Lives of Quiet Desperation: Divorced

Women with Children" (Berkeley: University of California, 1984). UMI Order No. 84-26895, 353-4.

> . . .the mothers who feel least isolated as single parents are the two who share parenting with their former husbands and four others whose children's fathers see them regularly and frequently. Although eight other fathers generally visit their children several times a month. . .these visits do not provide the mothers substantial relief from child care or parenting responsibilities. Nor do these fathers provide emotional support for parenting.

11. Michael E. Lamb, ed., *Nontraditional Families: Parenting and Child Development* (Hillsdale, NJ,: Lawrence Erlbaum Associates), 1982.

12. See Judy E. Nathan, "Visitation After Adoption: In the Best Interests of the Child," *New York University Law Review*, Vol. 59 (June 1984), 633-675. Nathan argues that the merits of access rights of biological parents with their children even exist after adoption.

13. See Hess and Camara, *op. cit.*, 91-92, for an explicit rebuttal of this idea: ". . .it appears that parental harmony is less important for most outcome variables than are the affective relationships that are maintained after divorce between the child and his or her parents. Only on the measure of stress was parental discord most important. For other outcome variables, the unique effects of parent-child interaction were larger than the unique contribution of the level of harmony between the two parents. Apparently, it is the quality of relationship between the child and parents that is most crucial in divorced families."

14. See Lublin, *op. cit.*, who found that fathers who saw their children more were also more loving with them. She speculates that "these fathers allowed themselves to experience the love they feel for their children; they are less haunted by the thought that their child will forget them. As they see the child more, they are most likely not as worried about the loss of connection as those fathers who see their children rarely. Hence, these fathers maintain the strong emotional bond." (106)

See also Carol R. Lowery and Shirley A. Settle, "Effects of Divorce on Children: Differential Impact of Custody and Visitation Patterns," *Family Relations*, October, 1985. Lowrey and Settle conclude that current custody and visitation decisions "are made according to fairly rigid, conventionalized standards. . .that poorly accommodate the variety of circumstances among individual families in minimizing stressful changes. . .the family systems literature suggests that continuity in the parenting role would minimize the demand on the children to develop new ways of interacting with their father." (458) The authors also review the factors which foster visitation by fathers without custody: "It seems that key factors may be to ensure that the father has easy access to his children and input into his children's lives, both of which are frequently denied fathers in actual practice. The current typical pattern for visitation seems to be weekends together, every other week. Bimonthly contact is generally considered "reasonable" visitation and constitutes the norm." (460-1)

See also Jerry W. McCant, "The Cultural Contradictions of Fathers as Non-parents," *Family Law Quarterly*, Vol. 21, No.1 (Spring 1987), 133-4.

15. Julie A. Fulton, "Parental Reports of Children's Post-divorce Adjustment," *Journal of Social Issues*, Vol. 35 No. 4 (1979), 126-139. See also Grossman, *op. cit.*, 132, 149, 153; and Novinson, *op. cit.*, 172.

16. McCant, *op. cit.*

17. See Greer Litton Fox, "Noncustodial Fathers," in *Dimensions of Fatherhood*, ed. Shirley Hanson and Frederick Bozett (Sage, 1985). See also Suzanne Bianchi and Judith Seltzer, "Life Without Father," *American Demographics*, December 1986, 43-7.

18. See Angela Stewart, *Characteristics of Parents Affecting Outcome of Court-Ordered Child Custody Mediation* (Doctoral Dissertation, American University), 1982. UMI Order No. 86-3929. Stewart found the use of mediation in a group of families resulted in significantly more satisfied parents, more amicable and less costly settlements, and more joint custody than in a control group whose settlements were not mediated. Also see the dissertation by Robert Moore (The Fielding Institute, 1984).

See also Robert Brien Moore, *Making the Peace: A Comparative Analysis of Divorce Mediation and the Traditional Legal Approach to Divorce* (Doctoral Dissertation, The Fielding Institute, 1984). UMI Order No. 85-6747.

19. See Robert Neil Califano, *Divorce Mediation: Clients' Perception of the Process* (Doctoral Dissertation, Saybrook Institute, 1987). UMI Order No. 87-21014, at 55, 137. See also Donald Strangio, *Characteristics of Parents Affecting Court-Ordered Child Custody Mediation* (Doctoral Dissertation, Univ. of San Francisco, 1986). UMI Order No. 87-13283, at 152-155.

20. Cochran, *op. cit.* Cochran favors joint physical custody, based on children's needs for expansive access to both parents; but he favors a presumption for sole legal custody in the "primary caretaker." The result of following Cochran's recommendation would be to recognize (and foster, where it might not have existed prior to divorce) a far more equal sharing of all parenting responsibilities than the "primary caretaker" standard implies. The concept of "primary caretaker" also presumes the superiority of different parenting roles. Also, so long as women are discriminated against in the economic world (work less or for less money), men will generally be discriminated against in assessing their relative contribution to parenting (men are less able for financial reasons to take time off work during the time their children are infants, hence are not usually "primary caretakers"). Yet, recent research on fathers

and fathering (see, for example, works by Michael Lamb; or Parke and Searle, "Fathering, It's a Major Role," in *Psychology Today*, Vol. 108, Nov. 1977) does not conclude that fathers or fathering are in any way less significant forms of parenting than mothers or mothering. Also, see Peter Neubauer, "Reciprocal Effects of Fathering on Parent and Child," in *Men Growing Up* (1986); Nathalie Martin, "Fathers and Families: Expanding the Familial Rights of Men," *Syracuse Law Review* Vol. 356 (1986), 1265-1302; Michael S. Kimmel, "Real Man Redux," *Psychology Today*, July 1987, 48-52. The concept of "primary caretaker" is one that may be more a measure of parental identification with the child than of the mother or father's parenting ability or commitment.

21. Ken Magid, "Children of Divorce: A Need for Guidelines," *Family Law Quarterly*, Vol. 20 No. 3 (Fall 1986), 331-341.

22. Lowery and Settle, *op. cit.*

23. See "The 1985 Virginia Slims American Women's Opinion Poll," 54.

24. *Marriage and Divorce Today*, Vol. 10, No. 41 (May 13, 1985).

25. Janine Schaub, *Joint Custody After Divorce: Views and Attitudes of Mental Health Professionals and Writers* (Doctoral Dissertation, Rutgers University, 1986). UMI Order No. 86-14559.

Chapter 4: Parenting Agreements—Preventive Medicine

1. William J. Bennett, speech to community groups, Omni Shoreham Hotel, Washington, DC, June 10, 1986. See *The Washington Post*, June 11, 1986. CRC was advised by the Department of Education that Bennett's remarks were based on statistical research articles appearing in *Principal* magazine, September 1982.

2. Peter Nash Swisher, "Divorce Planning in Antenuptial Agreements: Toward a New Objectivity," *University of Richmond Law Review*, Vol. 13, No. 2 (Winter 1979).

3. *Ibid.*

Chapter 5: Help for Families in Crisis

1. For more information, see "Review of Child Support Guidelines," CRC Report R115. Presents alternative approaches to financial child support guidelines based on federal and state sources. For use by advocates and legislators seeking equitable child support.

2. The four tax advantages that flow to the custodial parent are:

1. Favorable "head of household" treatment,
2. Child support taxable to the payor, tax-free to the payee.
3. The child exemption, worth $2,050 in 1992.
4. Child-care expenses.

3. E. J. Espenshade, *Investing in Children* (Washington, D.C.: Urban Institute, 1984).

4. See Margaret Creasy Ciardella, "*Plott v Plott*: Use of a Formula to Determine Child Support Obligations—A Continuation of Inconsistent and Inequitable Decisions?" *North Carolina Law Review*, Vol. 64 (August 1986), 1378-1394.

5. *Ibid.,* 1385.

6. *Ibid.*, 1383.

7. Espenshade, *op. cit.*; Lawrence Olson, *Costs of Children* (Lexington, MA: Lexington Books, 1983); Boone A. Turchi, *The Demand for Children: The Economics of Fertility in the United States* (Cambridge: Ballinger, 1975).

8. Paul Wise, "Correspondence," *Case and Comment*, May/June, 1981, 66.

9. David L. Levy, "Report to the Governor: Minority Report," Child Support Enforcement Advisory Council, Annapolis, MD. , September 1, 1986.

10. Robert G. Williams, "Development of Guidelines for Child Support Orders: Advisory Panel Recommendations and Final Report," Denver, CO, September 1987. Prepared at Policy Studies, Inc., under a grant to the National Center for State Courts, by the U.S. Office of Child Support Enforcement, U.S. Department of Health and Human Services.

11. See Domestic Relations Title 26.19.100 Appendix, Washington State Child Support Schedule, 1992.
12. Turchi, *op. cit.*, 218.

13. Levy, *op. cit.*, 7.

14. Susan Anderson-Khleif, *Divorced but not Disastrous: How to Improve the Ties Between Single-Parent Mothers, Divorced Fathers, and the Children* (Prentice-Hall, 1982), 148-150.

15. 626 2d 342, 290, 675.

16. 392 A.2d 1149, 40 Md. App. 550.

17. State of Michigan "Friend of the Court Act," 552.503.

Selected Research
on Child Custody

Research on child custody that is comprehensive in nature, based on true national samples, and presented objectively in both professional journals and the mass media, simply does not exist. However, numerous small but well-done studies have been available for many years. These studies, when carefully analyzed on a study-by-study basis and when considered as a group, provide a sound basis on which to formulate laws and public policy dealing with custody.

Many of the studies that CRC has relied on to formulate its policy of favoring a presumption of joint custody are summarized below in chronological order. It is obvious from this that even in the early 1980s joint custody had been established as being of greater benefit to children than sole custody.

1. Roman, 1978, in an analysis of 40 joint custody families and 60 sole custody families with varying custodial arrangements, found that children of joint custody were "thriving," not just "adjusting."

2. Nunan, 1980, compared 20 joint custody children between the ages of 7-11 with 20 age-matched children in sole custody, all from families which had been divorced or separated at least two years. However, for children four or older at time of separation, joint-custody children were found to have higher ego strengths, superego strengths, and self-esteem and were less excitable and impatient than their sole-custody counterparts. For children under four at the time of separation, there were no differences.

3. Luepnitz, 1980, studied joint-, maternal-, and paternal-custody families. Most single-parent children were found to be dissatisfied with the amount of visitation they had, whereas the joint-custody children were content with their arrangements. The quality of time spent with parents differed between the groups. The joint-custody children

retained a normal parent-child relationship, whereas sole-custodial children had a relationship with their non-custodial parent similar to a relationship between a child and an aunt or uncle. Joint-custody parents were less likely to feel overburdened by parenting responsibilities as compared to sole-custody parents.

4. Welsh-Osga, 1981, compared children aged 4½ to 10 years in intact families, as well as joint-, maternal-, and paternal-custody families. Children in all four groups were found to be equally well-adjusted on the various standardized measures used. Children from joint-custody families were more satisfied with the time spent with both parents than children from intact-, maternal-, and paternal-custody families. Parents in joint-custody families were significantly more involved in their children's critical life events than were sole-custody parents.

5. Karp, 1982, compared children aged 5-12 years in joint- and sole-custody as well as intact families. This study is unique because the parents had been separated for three months or less, whereas other studies assess adjustment two or more years after separation. Results indicated that girls in joint custody had significantly higher self-esteem than girls in sole custody. Boys and girls in single custody had significantly more negative involvement with their parents than did children in intact families. However, this was not true for children of joint custody. There was also an increase in sibling rivalry when sole-custody children were visiting with the non-custodial parent.

6. Cowan, 1982, compared 20 sole-maternal- and 20 joint-custody families. It was found that the more time children spent with their mothers, the more rejecting both parents were perceived to be, and the less well-adjusted were the children. The more time children spent with their fathers, the more accepting both parents were perceived to be, and the more well-adjusted were the children. Children in joint physical custody were rated as better adjusted by their mothers, were less likely to blame the father for the divorce, and had parents who were more supportive of each other.

7. Pojman, 1982, compared adjustment of boys aged 5-13 years in sole maternal custody, joint custody, happy marriages, and unhappy marriages. Boys in joint custody were significantly better adjusted than boys in sole custody and looked much like boys in happy families.

8. Livingston, 1983, compared children in sole-maternal, sole-pater-

nal, joint custody with mother as primary residential parent, and joint custody with father as primary residential parent. Children in joint custody—both boys and girls—were found to be better adjusted.

9. Patrician, 1984, investigated the extent to which conflict between parents is encouraged by unequal legal recognition of parental rights. Ninety fathers imagined themselves in one of three situations—non-custodial, custodial, or joint-legal custodial parent. Joint-legal custody was found to encourage concern for parental cooperation and discourage self-interest. Sole-custodial and non-custodial status encouraged punishment-oriented persuasion strategies. Unequal legal-custody power inhibits interparental cooperation, whereas equal legal-custody power facilitates interparental cooperation.

10. Shiller, 1984, compared 20 boys aged 6-11 years in joint custody to 20 age-matched boys in sole-maternal custody. Interviews with the boys as well as both parents were held. A number of tests were administered which indicated boys from joint-custody families were better adjusted than boys from maternal-custody families.

11. Granite, 1985, studied children aged 9-12 years in 15 joint-, 15 maternal-, and 15 paternal-custody families. While there were no differences among the three groups of children in self-concept, there were differences in the way the children perceived their parents. In both types of sole-custody homes, the custodial parent (both mothers and fathers) were perceived as using psychological pressure techniques to control children such as inducing guilt and intruding in their children's peer relationships. However, in joint-custody homes, where the responsibility for children was shared equally, children did not significantly perceive their parents as using psychological pressure techniques to control or interact with them.

12. Bredefeld, 1985, studied the effects of remarriage on physical joint- and sole-custodial mothers and their children. Both sole- and joint-custody children adjusted well to the remarriage of their mothers, with no significant differences found between the two groups. However, joint-custody couples expressed more satisfaction with their children as well as indicating that they appreciated the time alone with their new spouses. Sole-custody children more frequently reported their father saw them less often as a result of the remarriage of their mother than did joint-custody children.

13. Handley, 1985, studied latency age children in sole and joint

custody. Joint-custody children were more satisfied with their living arrangements and less likely to have a sense of loss and deprivation compared to sole-custody children.

14. Noonan, 1985, studied the effect of long-term conflict on personality function of children in joint-custody, sole-custody and intact families. Children in joint custody were significantly more active than children in intact families and in sole custody. Children in certain low-conflict situations demonstrated considerably less withdrawal in joint-custody families than in sole-custody and intact families.

15. Raines, 1985, describes a survey of over 1,200 children whose parents were divorcing. It was found 90 percent of children under the age of eight had a strong desire to live with both parents, 76 percent between eight and 10 wished to live with both parents, 44 percent between the ages of 10 and 12 wished to do so and only 20 percent between 14 and 16 would desire to live with both parents.

16. Wolchik, Braver, and Sandler, 1985, compared children in sole-maternal custody, joint physical custody, joint custody with mother as primary residential parent, and joint custody with father as primary residential parent. Children in joint custody reported significantly more positive experiences than children in maternal custody. Self-esteem was higher for children in joint custody.

17. Hanson, 1986, investigated 42 healthy single-parent families— 21 joint and 21 sole-custody families. Hanson found joint custody arrangements contribute positively to the mental health of mothers. Mothers with sole custody of sons had the least amount of social support, and mothers with joint custody of sons had the most. Custody arrangements have an effect on parent-child problem-solving with mothers reporting better problem-solving than fathers and joint-custody mothers reporting the best problem-solving of all.

18. Pearson and Thoennes, 1986, compared child-support payments by various sole-and joint-custodial configurations. Fathers with joint legal and residential custody, who were ordered to pay child support, had the best record of payment with a 95-percent compliance rate. Fathers with children in sole-maternal custody arrangements had the lowest compliance rate with 65 percent. Fathers with joint legal custody but maternal residential arrangements had a 90-percent compliance rate.

19. Isaacs, Leon, Kline, 1987, compared children in five custodial

groups—joint physical, joint legal-maternal, joint legal-paternal, sole maternal, and sole paternal to learn how children perceive their non-custodial and non-residential parents in relation to their other family members. On the measurement used, sole-custody children were three times more likely to omit one parent than the joint custody children.

20. Williams, 1987, compared children of joint and sole custody in high-conflict, high-risk situations. He found children in sole custody to be at greater risk for parental kidnapping and physical harm than children in joint custody. He also found that high-conflict families—either joint or sole custody—do better and are more likely to learn cooperation when they have comprehensive, highly detailed orders which leave little or nothing open to negotiation. He points out that none of the research to date on highly conflicted families has analyzed this group from the highly detailed nothing-left-to-negotiation order versus the little detailed a-lot-left-to-negotiation order.

21. Maccoby, Depner, and Mnookin, 1988, found joint-physical-custody children's parents had significantly less difficulty finding time to be with their children than did sole-custodial parents. Mothers with joint physical custody were more satisfied with their custody arrangements than sole custodial mothers where fathers visited.

22. Lehrman, 1990, compared 90 children aged 7 to 12 divided equally among maternal, joint legal, and joint physical custody groups. Joint-physical and joint-legal custody children had significantly fewer emotional behavioral problems than did the sole-custody subjects. Sole-custody children had greater self-hate and perceived more rejection from their fathers than joint-physical-custody children.

23. Pearson and Thoennes, 1990, while they did not find custody to be significant in explaining adjustment, did find regular visitation to be significant in a number of factors explaining positive adjustment patterns.

24. Bisnaire, Firestone, and Rynard, 1990, found visitation to be a significant factor in enabling children to maintain predivorce academic standards. Most dissertations comparing various aspects of joint and sole custody are not published in journals, but they are readily available from University Microfilms International, 300 North Zeeb Road, Ann Arbor, MI 48106, or by calling toll free 1-800-521-3042, and referencing the UMI Order No. appearing in the bibliography.

The best review of joint custody published to date is Joan B. Kelly's 1988 paper (see number 9 below) appearing in the *Journal of Family Psychology*. It is strongly recommended that advocates become thoroughly familiar with her review.

1) Bisnaire, L.M.C., Firestone, P., and Rynard, D. (1990). Factors associated with academic achievement in children following parental separation. *American Journal of Orthopsychiatry*, 60(1), 67-76.

2) Bredefeld, G.M. (1985). Joint custody and remarriage: its effects on marital adjustment and children. Doctoral dissertation, California School of Professional Psychology, Fresno. UMI Order No. 85-10926.

3) Cowan, D.B. (1982). Mother custody versus joint custody: Children's parental relationship and adjustment. Doctoral dissertation, University of Washington. UMI Order No. 82-18213.

4) Granite, B.H. (1985). An investigation of the relationship among self-concept, parental behaviors, and the adjustment of children in different custodial living arrangements following a marital separation and/or a divorce. Doctoral dissertation, University of Pennsylvania, Philadelphia. UMI Order No. 85-23424.

5) Handley, S. (1985). The experience of the child in sole and joint custody. The experience of the latency age child in sole and joint custody: A report on a comparative study. Doctoral dissertation, California Graduate School of Marriage and Family Therapy.

6) Hanson, S.M.H. (1985). Healthy single parent families. *Family Relations*, 35, 125-132.

7) Isaacs, M.B., Leon, G.H., Kline, M. (1987). When is a parent out of the picture? Different custody, different perceptions. *Family Process*, 26, 101-110.

8) Karp, E.B. (1982). Children's adjustment in joint and single custody: An empirical study. Doctoral dissertation, California School of Professional Psychology, Berkeley. UMI Order No. 83-6977.

9) Kelly, J.B. (1988). Longer-term adjustment in children of divorce: Converging Findings and Implications for Practice. *Journal of Family Psychology*, 2, 119-140.

10) Kline, M., Tschann, J.M., Johnston, J.R., & Wallerstein, J.S.

(1989). Children's adjustment in joint and sole physical custody families. *Developmental Psychology*, 25, 430-435.

11) Livingston, J.A. (1983). Children after divorce; A psychosocial analysis of the effects of custody on self-esteem. Doctoral dissertation, University of Vermont. UMI Order No. 83-26981.

12) Luepnitz, D.A. (1980). Maternal, paternal, and joint custody: A study of families after divorce. Doctoral dissertation, State University of New York at Buffalo. UMI Order No. 80-27618.

13) Luepnitz, D.A. (1982). Child Custody: A study of families after divorce. Lexington, MA: Lexington Books.

14) Maccoby, E.E., Mnookin, R.H., and Depner, C.E. (1986, May). Post-divorce families: Custodial arrangements compared. Paper presented at the meeting of the American Association of Science, Philadelphia.

15) Noonan, L.P. (1985). Effects of long-term conflict on personality functioning of children of divorce. Doctoral dissertation, The Wright Institute Graduate School of Psychology, Berkeley, CA. UMI Order No. 84-17931.

16) Nunan, S.A. (1980). Joint custody versus single custody effects on child development. Doctoral dissertation, California School of Professional Psychology, Berkeley. UMI Order No. 81-10142.

17) Patrician, M.R. (1984). The effects of legal child-custody status on persuasion strategy, choices, and communication goals of fathers. Doctoral dissertation, University of San Francisco. UMI Order No. 85-14995.

18) Pearson, J. and Thoennes, N. (1986). Will this divorced woman receive child support? Your custody decision may determine the answer. *The Judges Journal*, Winter, 1986.

19) Pearson, J. and Thoennes, N. (1990). Custody after divorce: Demographic and attitudinal patterns. *American Journal of Orthopsychiatry*, 60(2), 233-249.

20) Pojman, E.G. (1982). Emotional adjustment of boys in sole custody and joint custody compared with adjustment of boys in happy

and unhappy marriages. Unpublished doctoral dissertation, California Graduate Institute, Los Angeles.

21) Raines, P.M. (1986). Joint custody and the right to travel: legal and psychological implications. *Journal of Family Law*, June 1986, 24, 625-656.

22) Roman, M. and Haddad, W. (1978). The case for joint custody. *Psychology Today*, September 1978, 96.

23) Shiller, V. (1984). Joint and Maternal custody: The outcome for boys aged 6-11 and their parents. Doctoral dissertation, University of Delaware. UMI Order No. 85-11219.

24) Shiller, V. (1986). Joint versus maternal families with latency age boys: Parent characteristics and child adjustment. *American Journal of Orthopsychiatry*, 56, 486-489.

25) Welsh-Osga, B. (1981). The effects of custody arrangements on children of divorce. Doctoral dissertation, University of South Dakota. UMI Order No. 82-6914.

26) Williams, F.S. (1987). Child custody and parental cooperation. Paper presented at American Bar Association Family Law Section, August 1987 and January 1988.

27) Wolchik, Sharlene A., Braver, Sanford L. and Sandler, Irwin N. Maternal versus joint custody: Children's post separation experiences and adjustment. *Journal of Clinical Child Psychology*, 1985, 14, 5-10.

State Laws Addressing Child Custody

Alabama. Marital and Domestic Relations Sec. 30-3-1, Code of Alabama. No joint custody statute; no preference for either father or mother in custody. Joint custody permitted by case law, see Simmons v Simmons, 422 S.2d. 799; and ex parte Couch, 521 S.2d 987.

Alaska. Marital and Domestic Relations Sec. 25.20.060. Shared custody may be awarded if determined by the court to be in the best interest of the child.

Arizona. Marital and Domestic Relations Sec. 25-322. Joint custody is an option if either both parents agree or if one parent requests it.

Arkansas. Family Law Sec. 9-13-101. No joint custody provisions; however, there is no parental preference in custody. Joint custody permitted by case law, see Childers v O'Neal, 251 Arkansas 1097; Drewry v Drewry, 3 Ark. App. 97.

California. Family Law Sec. 4600.5. Presumption for joint custody if both parents agree, and an option if they do not agree. Policy statement states that children shall have "frequent and continuing contact" with both parents; a factor in granting custody shall be which parent is most likely to foster close contact with the other parent.

Colorado. Domestic Matters Sec. 14-10-123.5. Joint custody is an option upon request of either party or by motion of the court.

Connecticut. Family Law Sec. 46B-56A. Presumption for joint custody if both parents agree.

Delaware. Domestic Relations 13 Sec. 722. Joint custody is statutorily implied.

Florida. Civil Procedure and Practice Sec. 61-13. A presumption for shared parental responsibility.

Georgia. Domestic Relations Sec. 19-9-3 and Sec. 19-9-6. Option for joint custody.

Hawaii. Family Courts 571-46.1. Upon the application of either parent, joint custody may be awarded.

Idaho. Domestic Relations 32-717B. Presumption for legal and physical joint custody.

Illinois. Domestic Relations 40 Sec. 602.1. Upon the application of either or both parents or upon its own motion, the court may consider joint custody.

Indiana. Marriage and Divorce. 31-1-11.5-21. The court may award joint legal custody.

Iowa. Domestic Relations Sec. 598.41. Presumption for joint legal and physical custody.

Kansas. Divorce and Maintenance 60-1610. Preference for joint legal and physical custody.

Kentucky. Domestic Relations 403-270. Option for joint custody.

Louisiana. Husband and wife Civil Code Art. 131. Presumption for joint legal and physical joint custody.

Maine. Domestic Relations 19-752. Shared parenting is a presumption if both parents agree, and an option if they do not.

Maryland. Family Law 5-203. An option for joint custody.

Massachusetts. Domestic Relations 208, Sec. 31. A presumption for shared legal custody at temporary hearing; at permanent hearing, shared parenting an option if one parent requests it.

Michigan. Domestic Relations Secs. 25.312 (3) through 25.312 (6). Joint custody is a presumption if parents agree, an option if they do not.

Minnesota. Domestic Relations Sec. 518-17. A presumption for joint legal and physical custody.

Mississippi. Domestic Relations Sec. 983-5-24. A preference for joint legal and physical custody.

Missouri. Domestic Relations 452.370. Preference for joint legal and physical custody.

Montana. Family Law 40-4-222. A preference for joint legal and physical custody.

Nebraska. Husband and Wife Sec. 42-363. An option for joint custody.

New Hampshire. Domestic Relations Sec. 458:17. A presumption for joint legal custody if the parents agree and an option if they do not.

New Jersey. Children-Juvenile and Domestic Relations Courts 912-2. An option for joint custody.

New Mexico. Domestic Affairs Sec. 40-4-9.1. A presumption for joint legal and physical custody.

New York. Domestic Relations Law Art. 5, C70.1. There is no mention of custody types, either sole or joint. Joint custody is permitted by case law, sometimes over the objections of a parent. Sussman v Sussman, 494 New York Supp.2d 924; and Martin v Martin, 493 New York Supp.2d 840.

North Carolina. Divorce Sec. 13.2. An option for joint custody.

North Dakota. Domestic Relations and Persons Sec. 14-09-06.1.

Ohio. Domestic Relations—Children Sec. 3109.04. An option for shared parenting (joint custody).

Oklahoma. Marriage and Family Sec. 43-109. A preference for joint custody.

Oregon. Domestic Relations 107.169. A presumption for joint custody only when both parents agree; otherwise an option.

Pennsylvania. Domestic Relations Sec. 23 Pa.C.S.A. Sec. 5301, 5302, 5303. An option for shared parenting.

Rhode Island. Domestic Relations Sec. 15-5-16. No joint custody statute; joint custody permitted by case law, see Loebenberg v Loebenberg, 127 Atlantic 2d 500, 1956; Zinni v Zinni, 238 Atlantic 2d 373, 1968.

South Carolina. Domestic Relations Sec. 20-3-160. There is no mention of custody types, either sole or joint. Case law is extremely restrictive of joint custody—appears to prohibit joint physical custody, Mixon v Mixon, 171 S.E.2d 581, 1969.

South Dakota. Domestic Relations Sec. 25-5-7.1. An option for joint custody.

Tennessee. Domestic Relations 36-6-101. An option for joint custody.

Texas. Family Code Sec. 14.01. An option for joint custody (joint managing conservatorship). But note that Texas law (Sec. 14.033) requires that a judge must give a parent at least 34 percent of the time with the child. A judge may give more but not less time, absent good reason, to be stated in writing.

Utah. Divorce 30.3-10.1. A presumption for joint legal custody. No mention of physical custody types.

Vermont. Domestic Relations T.15 Sec. 665. By statute, the court may order rights and responsibilities to be shared between the parents if they agree. When the parents cannot agree, the court will award parental rights and responsibilities primarily or solely to one parent.

Virginia. Domestic Relations Sec. 20.1072. An option for joint custody.

Washington (state). Domestic Relations 2609.184. The criteria for the parenting plan required of divorcing parents implies the acceptability of joint custody.

West Virginia. Domestic Relations Sec. 48-215. No provisions for joint custody. Custody goes to the primary caretaker—the individual who takes care of the child's day to day needs. Joint custody is permissible by case law when the parent determined by the court to be the primary caretaker agrees to it. In those rare cases where the court cannot distinguish between the parents as to whom the primary caretaker is, the court may order joint custody over the opposition of one or both parents. See Lowe v Lowe, 370 S.E.2d 731, 1988; David M. v Margaret M., 385 S.E.2d 912, 1989; Loedermilk v Loedermilk, 397 S.E.2d 905, W. Va. 990.

Wisconsin. Actions Affecting the Family, 767.24. Joint legal custody is an option if one or both parents request it. The court allocates physical custody.

Wyoming. Dissolution of Marriage, Sec. 20-2-113. No joint custody provisions; however, parents have been granted joint physical and legal custody when both agree to it.

Washington, D.C. Divorce, Annulment, Separation, Support, etc., 16-911. No joint custody statute, no preference for either father or mother in custody. However, the child support guidelines in 16-916.1 (n) state that "In a case in which shared custody is ordered or agreed to, and the child spends 40% or more of the child's time with each parent. . ." implies that joint custody is an option whether or not the parents agree.

Puerto Rico. Affects of Divorce, T.31, Sec. 383. No joint custody provision, no preference for either parent.

Virgin Islands. Domestic Relations, T.16, Sec. 109. Custody types are not statutorily mentioned. By case law, the courts are considered to have the right to grant joint custody when parents agree to and in rare cases when they don't, see Charles v Charles, Terr. Ct. St. C. 1987, 23 V.I. 103.

About CRC

The Children's Rights Council (CRC), also known as the National Council for Children's Rights, is a non-profit [IRS 501(c)3] organization, based in Washington, D.C. We are concerned with the healthy development of children of divorced and separated parents. For the child's benefit, we seek means of reducing divorce by strengthening families through divorce and custody reform, minimizing hostilities between parents who are involved in marital disputes, substituting conciliation and mediation for the adversarial approach, assuring a child's access to both parents, and providing equitable child support.

CRC was founded in 1985 by concerned parents who have more than 40 years collective experience in divorce reform and early childhood education.

Prominent professionals in the fields of religion, law, social work, psychology, child care, education, business and government comprise our Advisory Panel.

For further information about membership, publications, cassettes, catalog, and services, write: CRC, 220 "I" Street, NE, Washington, DC 20002, or call 1-800-787-KIDS or (202) 547-6227. Our fax number is (202) 546-4CRC (4272).

OFFICERS:
David L. Levy, Esq., President
Anna Keller, Vice President
John L. Bauserman, VP/Treasurer
Ellen Dublin Levy, Secretary

HONORARY PRESIDENT:
David Brenner, Entertainer
New York, New York

GENERAL COUNSEL:
Michael L. Oddenino
Arcadia, California

DIR. OF INFORMATION SERVICES:
Ed Mudrak

DIRECTOR OF PUBLICATIONS:
Deanne Mechling

DIRECTOR OF DEVELOPMENT:
Clifton A. Clark

ADVISORY PANEL:
Rabbi Mendel Abrams, D. Min.
Former President, Board of Rabbis
of Greater Washington, DC

Sam Brunelli, Executive Director
American Legislative Exchange Council
Washington, D.C.

Stuart W. Cochran II
Elkhart, Indiana

Jim Cook, President
Joint Custody Association
Los Angeles, California

"Dear Abby"
(Abigail Van Buren)
Los Angeles, California

Honorable Dennis DeConcini
U.S. Senator, Arizona

Karen DeCrow
Former President of N.O.W.
Jamesville, New York

Elliott H. Diamond
Co-Founder, CRC
Reston, Virginia

Ethel Dunn, Executive Director
Grandparents United for Children's Rights

Honorable David Durenberger
U.S. Senator, Minnesota

Meyer Elkin, Co-Founder
Association of Family & Conciliation Courts
Beverly Hills, California

Warren Farrell, Ph.D., Author,
Former Member of the Board of
Directors New York City N.O.W.
Leucadia, California

Doris Jonas Freed, Esq., Co-Chair
New York State Bar Association Family Law
Section's Custody Committee
New York, New York

Larry Gaughan, Law Professor,
Professional Director, Family Mediation
of Greater Washington, D.C.

Ronald T. Haskins, Ph.D.
Associate Director, Bush Institute for Child and
Family Policy, University of North Carolina,
Chapel Hill (1978-85)

Jennifer Isham, President
Mothers Without Custody (MW/OC)
Crystal Lake, Illinois

Joan Berlin Kelly, Ph.D.
Executive Director
Northern California Mediation Center

Elisabeth Kübler-Ross, M.D.
Author, Psychiatrist
Head Waters, Virginia

Vicki Lansky, Author/Columnist
Deephaven, Minnesota

James Levine, The Fatherhood Project
The Bank Street College of Education
New York, New York

Dr. Carl H. Mau, Jr.
General Secretary (1974-85)
Lutheran World Federation
Geneva, Switzerland

John Money, Ph.D., Professor of
Medical Psychology and Pediatrics
Johns Hopkins University and Hospital
Baltimore, Maryland

Sue Klavans Simring
Co-Director, Family Solutions
The Center of Divorce and Custody Consultation
Englewood, New Jersey

Debbie Stabenow
State Senate, Michigan

CRC Chapters and Affiliates

(as of February 1, 1993)
For further information, contact CRC at
202-547-6227 or 1-800-787-KIDS

CRC seeks to form chapters throughout the country, in order to assist the citizens of each state with that state's unique laws. Custody reform is primarily handled on the state level, although Congress is entering the field more and more. Problems cross state lines. What happens in one state or in Congress affects all of us. We must have a strong national organization, with strong state organizations, to have greater effect on public policy.

If you are part of a national network, you will generally get a better reception than a group that is limited to one state or community.

Coordinators of our state chapters maintain contact by mail exchange and cross-country telephone conference calls between the chapters and CRC national. In this way, chapters can benefit from each other and do not have to constantly "re-invent the wheel".

Chapters exist in 23 states.

If you live in a state where there is a CRC chapter, we urge you to join the chapter. In this way, you will be networking work with a chapter and national CRC to reform custody law and attitudes around the country. By becoming a member of the chapter, you also become a member of national CRC.

If you would like to learn if a chapter is forming in your state, or if you would like to form a chapter in your own state or community, write to CRC for our Affiliation Booklet.

This 37-page booklet explains everything you want to know about affiliation.

After reviewing the booklet, write to Eric Anderson of Texas, CRC chapter coordinator, for further information. Eric's address is listed below.

Note: CRC's name is protected by federal trademark law.

National Affiliate Organizations

Grandparents United for Children's Rights (GUCR)
137 Larkin Street
Madison, WI 53705
Ethel Dunn, President
(608) 238-8751
GUCR has chapters
in more than 20 states

Mothers Without Custody (MW/OC)
P.O. Box 27418
Houston, TX 77227-7418
(713) 840-1626
Jennifer Isham, president
MW/OC has chapters in more
than 20 states

CRC Chapters

Alabama
CRC of Alabama
454 Morphy Ave.
Fairhope, AL 36532
(205) 928-0464
E.D. Wilson, coordinator

Alaska
Alaska Dads and Moms
2225 Arctic Boulevard, Ste 303
Anchorage, AK 99503
(907) 274-7358
Gary Maxwell, state coordinator

Alaska Family Support Group
P.O. Box 111691
Anchorage, AK 99511-1691
(907) 344-7707
Jim Arnesen, president

Second Wives and Children
P.O. Box 875731
Wasilla, AK 99687-5731
(907) 376-1445
Tracy Driskill, president

California
CRC of California and
San Francisco Chapter
2547 Noriega Street, Suite 333
San Francisco, CA 94122
(415) 753-8315
Lou Ann Bassan, coordinator

Children's Rights Council of
California, Sacramento Chapter
P. O. Box 60811
Sacramento, CA 95860
(916) 635-2590
Patricia Gehlen, chair

Colorado
Children's Rights Council of
Colorado
P. O. Box 280084
Lakewood, CO 80228
(303) 980-6903
Valerie Ozsu, coordinator

Delaware
Children's Rights Council of
Delaware
P.O. Box 182
Bethel, DE 19931
(302) 875-7353
Bill Barrall, coordinator
(302) 734-8522
James Morning, president

Florida
Florida CRC chapter
113 W. Tara Lakes Drive
Boynton Beach, FL 33436
1-800-787-KIDS
Piotr Blass, coordinator

Georgia
Georgia Council for Children's
Rights
P.O. Box 70486
Marietta, GA 30007-0486
(404) 928-7110
Sonny Burmeister, coordinator

Illinois
Children's Rights Council of
Illinois
P.O. Box 786
Pekin, IL 61555-0786
(309) 697-3235
Ann Danner, coordinator

Indiana
Indiana Council for Children's
Rights
2625 N. Meridian, Ste 202
Indianapolis, IN 46208
(317) 925-5433
David Dinn, coordinator

Iowa
Fathers for Equal Rights, Inc.
3623 Douglas Avenue
Des Moines, IA 50310
(515) 277-8789
Dick Woods, coordinator

Professionals Serving Custodial
and Non-Custodial Parents
(515) 264-9511
Eric Borseth, J.D.

Kansas/Missouri
Children's Rights Council of
Kansas and Missouri
5516 Mission Road
Fairway, KS 66205-2721
(913) 831-0190
Roger Doeren, coordinator

Kentucky
Children's Rights Council of
Kentucky
1645 Robin Road
Owensboro, KY 42301
(502) 684-6100
Tracy Cox, coordinator

Maryland
Children's Rights Council of
Maryland
417 Pershing Drive
Silver Spring, MD 20910

(301) 588-0262
Harvey Walden, coordinator

Massachusetts
Concerned Fathers of
Massachusetts, Inc.
P.O. Box 2768
Springfield, MA 01101-2768
(413) 736-7432
George Kelly, coordinator

Carla Goodwin, Divorce
Mediation
820 Washington Street
South Easton, MA 02375
(508) 238-3722

Michigan
Children's Rights Council of
Michigan
P.O. Box 416
Lawton, MI 49065-0416
(616) 247-5868
Heather Rowlison, coordinator

New Jersey
New Jersey Council for
Children's Rights (NJCCR)
P.O. Box 615
Wayne, NJ 07470-0615
(201) 694-9323
Erich Sturn, president

New York
Children's Rights Council of
New York
35 Front Street
Binghamton, NY 13905
(607) 785-9338
Kim Boedecker-Frey,
coordinator

Ohio
CRC of Ohio
9681 Harding Hwy. E.
Galion, OH 44833
(419) 845-2572
Kathy Clark, coordinator

Pennsylvania
P.E.A.C.E. (Parents Equality
and Children's Equality)
20½ S. Bradford St.
Allentown, PA 18103
(800) 787-KIDS
Gary Onuschak, coordinator

Texas
Texas Children's
Rights Coalition
(TCRC)
P.O. Box 12961
Capitol Station
Austin, TX 78711
(512) 499-TCRC
Eric Anderson, coordinator and
nationwide chapter coordinator

Vermont
Vermonters for
Strong Families
R.R. 1, Box 267A1,
Heartland, VT 05048
(802) 436-3089
Fred Tubbs, coordinator

Virginia
Children's Rights Council of
Tidewater
3029 Yakima Road
Chesapeake, VA 23325
(804) 463-KIDS
Michael Ewing, president
Cindy Lewis, state coordinator

Family Resolution Council
8935 Patterson Avenue
Richmond, VA 23229
(804) 740-9889
Murray Steinberg, president

Fathers United for
Equal Rights
and Women's Coalition
P.O. Box 1323
Arlington, VA 22210-1323
(703) 451-8580
Paul Robinson, president

Children's Rights Council

ALSO KNOWN AS

National Council for Children's Rights

We are proud of your achievements, CRC! Sign me up and send me the benefits listed below. Enclosed is my tax deductible contribution as a:

☐ New Member, $35
☐ Sustaining member, $60
☐ Sponsor, $125
☐ Life member, $500
☐ Other $_____
☐ I can't join now, but here is my tax-deductible
   contribution of $_____.

PLEASE CHECK ALL THAT APPLY.
☐ MC ☐ VISA CC#_____ Exp. date_____

CRC # _____ if renewal or change of address see CRC number
   on label.

Title_____(Mr., Ms., Dr., Rev., etc.)

Name_____

Suffix _____(ACSW, MD, etc.) Nickname _____(Optional)

Organization (48 Character max.)_____
_____

Delivery Address (48 Character max.): _____

City _____

State (2 characters)_____Zip Code _____
Country _____(If other than US.)

Organization phone _____

Home phone _____Work phone _____
If organization is listed in CRC Directory, organization phone
number will be listed.   (OVER)

(Home and work phone numbers are for CRC internal use only.)

Fax number _____

Chapter name, if affiliated with CRC _____

As a member, please send me *Speak Out For Children* (CRC's Quarterly Newsletter), Catalog of Resources (in which I receive discounts) and the following at NO ADDITIONAL COST:

• "A Child's Right - 2 Parents," Bumper Sticker.

• FREE! A $10 VALUE - A 32-page report, Written Preliminary Proceedings from CRC's 1993 Seventh National Conference (submitted prior to conference). Includes 18 different reports including Access Enforcement Programs, Recognizing Child Abuse, Access to Grandparents, How to Demilitarize Divorce.

☐ For membership or renewal of more than $35, send me a list of free items I'm entitled to (the higher the contributions, the more items that are free). If you are an individual member of CRC, your name may be given on occasion to other children's rights organizations, organizations that support CRC, or individuals seeking a referral for help. If you do not want your name to be given for these purposes, please check here . ☐

Call 1-800-787-KIDS or (202) 547-6227 to charge your membership to a credit card, or send completed form to CRC, 220 "I" Street, NE, Suite 230, Washington, DC 20002-4362.

If you live in AL, AK, AZ, CA, DE, FL, GA, IN, IA, IL, KS, KY, MA, MI, MO, MD, NJ, NY, OH, PA, TX, VA, VT, we ask that you join the CRC chapter in that state (which includes membership in CRC National). For address of chapter in those states, see elsewhere in this book, or write to CRC for information.